Illustration by David Delatorre

Disclaimer: We do not hold ourselves out as professional counselors. Neither is the material provided herein intended to serve as legal advice, nor does it derive from specialized training. Rather, our perspectives are solely based on *personal* experience, designed to uplift and inspire the general public.

Copyright ©Mordechai and Esther Fintz, 2021. All rights reserved.

This is a work of nonfiction. Any resemblance to or association with actual persons or locations are purely coincidental and unintentional.

No part of this book may be reproduced in any form, either in print, by electronic or other mechanical means whatsoever.

Contents

A PRACTICAL GUIDE TO PERSONAL AND MARITAL HAPPINESS

Acknowledgments xi
About the Authors 1
Introduction 3

Part I—How to Achieve Personal Success
   and Happiness 7

Chapter 1— Cleansing Your Past and Embracing a New
Beginning 9

(A) *Taking a Good Look At Yourself* 9
(B) *Establishing a Relationship with the Creator* 12

Chapter 2 — Beginning Each Day With An
Attitude of Gratitude 15

(A) *Expressing Your Gratitude* 15
(B) *There Is a Purpose In All Changes* 16
(C) *Following Gods "GPS"* 17
(D) Helpful Practices 18
(E) Reaching Out to Others 19
(F) The Two-Dollar Gift Certificate 19
(G) The "AY-YA-YA-YA-YAI!" Cheer 20

Self-Confidence

CONTENTS, CONTINUED...

Chapter 3 —Commiting to Daily Reading of
               Positive and Motivational Material 23

(A) *Relativity* 24
(B) *Troubles In the River* 25
(C) *Affirmation—Albert Camus* 26

Chapter 4 — Believe In Yourself 29

(A) *Get To Know Yourself Better* 29
(B) *Act In Furtherance of Your Potential* 30
(C) *Be the Co-creator of Your Destiny* 30
(D) *Do Not Be Afraid of Mistakes or Failures* 31
(E) *Avoid the Naysayers* 31
(F) *Claim Your Purpose, Accept Challenges, and
    Look For Possibilities* 32
(G) *The Difference Between Self-Belief
    and Arrogance* 32

Chapter 5 — Understanding the Law of Attraction 35

(A) *Your Thoughts and Visions* 36
(B) *Communication* 37
(C) Initiative and Action.. 38
    (*The Frog Anecdote*) 39
(D) *Your Outcome* 40

Chapter 6 — Treasuring Family and Others
               With Universal Love (Agape) 43

(A) *Compassion, Kindness, Respect, and Love
    Toward Others* 43
(B) *Demonstrate the Above Without Judgment* 46

Compassion

Contents, Continued . . .

Chapter 7 — Create a "Bucket List" — Dream Big!............. 47

(A) *Origin of the Term "Bucket List"*... 47
(B) *Creating Your Bucket List* 47
(C) *Dream Big!* 48
(D) *Live Each Day In Expectation of Your*
     Dreams' Fulfillment 49

Part II — Meeting Your Soul Mate and
             Preparing For Your Marriage 51

Understanding the General Distinctions Between
Male and Female Approaches... 53

Chapter 1 — The Definition of "Soul Mate" and
             How to Use the Law of Attraction toFind
             Your 'Kindred Spirit' 57

(A) *The Definition of "Soul Mate"* 57
(B) *How to Use the Law of Attraction*
     to Find Your 'Kindred Spirit' 58

(1) *Your Thoughts and Visions* 58
(2) *Communication* 59
(3) *Initiation and Action* 60
(4) *Your Outcome*.. 61

Kindness

Contents, Continued . . .

Chapter 2 — Habits and Practices That Foster
               a Healthy Relationship 63
(A) *Trust* 63
(B) *Reputation* 65
(C) *Reliability* 66
(D) *Supportiveness* 67
(E) *Communication* 67
     (The Message Game) 68
(F) *Respect* 69

The Elements of Respect 69

(1) *Tolerance/Understanding* 69
(2) *Awareness* 70
(3) *Security* 71
(3) *Validation* 71

The Relationship Between Love, Trust, and Respect 72

The Difference Between Behavior of the Flesh
and the Spirit 72

Chapter 3 — The Importance of Compromise
               and Open Communication 75

(1) Domestic Life 76

(A) *Chore Responsibilities* 76
(B) *Compromise* 77
(C) *The Significance of Honest Dialogue and*
    Mutual Understanding 78
    (The Spinach Pie Story) 78

Respect

CONTENTS, CONTINUED...

(2) The "You Matter" Commitment 80

(A) *Habits and Behaviors* 81
(1) *Commitment to Mutual Engagement In Life* 81
(2) *Learning About "Love Buttons"* 81
(3) *Validate Your Significant Other* 85
(4) *The "Matchy-Matchy" Challenge* 85
(5) *Intimacy and Sexual Practices* 86
(6) *Respecting Boundaries* 87
(7) *Apologize For Wrongdoing or*
    Unintentional Errors 89
(8) *Avoid Jealousy* 90

Chapter 4 — Family Life—Building Your
              Life Together 91

(A) *Establish Your Circle of Love and Build On*
    Your Circle of Life 92

(B) *Write Down Your Mutual Goals and Bucket Lists* 93
(C) *Use God's Personal Service ("GPS")*
    As Your Family Guide 95
(D) Wedding Tips 96
(E) Honeymoon Preparation — Suggestions 103
(F) Family Planning 107
(G) Help Your Children With Their Personal Growth 112
(H) Divorce 115

Conclusion — Final Thoughts and Synopsis 119
The Gratitude Prayer 123
Mordechai and Esther's Romantic Playlist 125

"It takes a village"

ACKNOWLEDGMENTS

When we heard the expression, "It takes a village to raise a child," we recalled how appropriate the phrase was in our own lives. When we had our son, we were young and fortunate to experience "the village" experience firsthand through our family's phenomenal support and cooperation.

The same holds true for the creative process, and we wish to acknowledge all of those who have made this book possible.

First and foremost, we thank God for providing us with the inspiration, experience, and determination to share our fifty-seven years of wisdom. We hope that this manual serves as a lasting foundation for beginning and continuing relationships, now and for years to come.

We are profoundly grateful for God's Personal Service ("GPS") on this beautiful journey called 'life.' We are mindful of the Creator's presence in everything we undertake, including this book, as well as our other books that address our favorite subjects: marriage, love, inspiration, success, abundance, peace, and happiness.

Friends and family make the world a better place

We wish to thank the following people who have contributed their time and love to this effort:

Gabriella Gafni, our editor, and friend, for providing inspiration and editorial assistance. We are very grateful that you are part of our team.

David Delatorre, our masterful cover-designer and illustrator, whose work receives universal admiration among our readers. Your constant support and contributions so beautifully enhance the presentation of our books.

Irving and Joanne Shulkes, loving friends who are our extended family and blessings from God. Thank you for your unwavering support, assistance, encouragement, and input on phraseology that saw us through to the completion of this text. Your comments below are noteworthy, and we are most grateful:

To Esther and Mordechai,
This is a very mature, well-thought-out, and beautifully written book.
May the work of your hands be blessed in all your endeavors.
Joanne & Irving Shulkes

Fela Fintz, when God brought you and Leon together, that was the most wonderful event for both of you and our entire family. We are so blessed to have you as our sister-

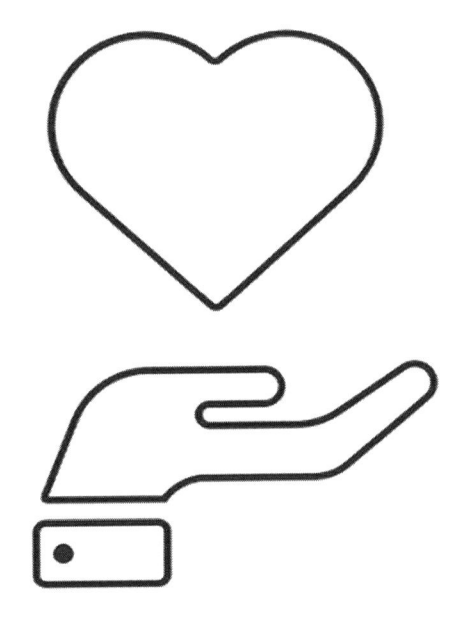

Thank you for your support

in-law. Your talent, proofreading, and translation skills are unmatched. Thank you and Leon for your continuous support in helping this book come to fruition.

Rachel Fresco, we thank you for your inspiration, resourcefulness, willingness to assist us with the production of this book, and proofreading.

Izzy, Janice, Mindy, Carlos, and Sara, Thank you for being the most beautiful family any two people can have, for your incredible support and love throughout the entire creative process and in every facet of our lives.

To All Our Unmentioned Family and Friends who have assisted us on this journey, we extend our blessings and heartfelt thanks.

God, family, and friends act as a trilogy to provide guidance and assistance in everyone's life. Look around and enhance your life and your goals by requesting help from those who care.

This book is a testament to a 'village' of hearts that makes all things possible.

@mordechiandesther
www.makelifeasuccess.com

...There Is No Esther Without
Mordechai and No Mordechai
Without Esther...Two Who Love, Motivate,
and Encourage Each Other to Become
All God Calls Them to Be

ABOUT THE AUTHORS

Mordechai and Esther Fintz are the authors of the acclaimed book, *What Makes Our Life a Success?* They are also song lyricists (Please visit their website at: **www.makelifeasuccess.com**). Their first book enabled them to launch their online course "Couples' Enlightenment Program" and a television series "Make Life a Success," aired from Atlanta, GA, and streaming channels on the web.

The authors are presently working on their "TLC" series of books with a view to uplifting and inspiring others and awakening them to God's presence in every individual's life. Most significantly, the Creator guides and sustains every married couple's life—just as God has empowered them to rejoice in fifty-seven years of marital bliss.

*Facing ourselves requires a leap of faith and the courage
to acknowledge that to err is human.*

INTRODUCTION

In our uncertain world, where we are either quarantining or interacting in different ways (e.g., by video-conferencing, phone, the Internet, or limited in-person contact), the act of looking within ourselves contributes to our success, happiness, and personal growth. Only when we understand who we are as individuals, establish a one-on-one relationship with God, confront our limitations and learn from our past mistakes will we be able to participate in a Circle of Love and society. Once we are willing to admit our mistakes, improve upon our past experiences, and turn our weaknesses and failings in a more positive direction, we are ready to reach out to meet our soul mate—the person we ultimately choose as our life partner— or spouse, in sickness or health, in wealth or poverty for the rest of our earthly life and into eternity.

This book guides our readers through a process of self-reflection—whether you practice a particular religion or do not adhere to a particular faith at all. You will find wisdom and strength in the examples and suggestions we provide in these pages, derived from our many years of experience in our personal and prosperous married life. With a commitment to full self-integration (*a complete understanding of the self*), you can be ready to expand your horizon— to live a happy life with success and purpose on earth and into eternity.

Facing ourselves requires a leap of faith and the courage to acknowledge that to err is human. There is no shame in stumbling, falling, dusting ourselves off, and casting away all the past experiences and negative influences that have hurt you. These forces have been implanted in our minds either by others around us or are self-inflicted. When we acknowledge them, we equip ourselves with enhanced knowledge and determination to live a harmonious, enjoyable life—even when we don't get exactly what we want. Only then can we move forward with a deeper understanding of life; only then can we maintain a harmonious, happy state of being. "Life is beautiful, and I am grateful for the ability to rejoice in this new day!"

Because personal and relationship development are two separate, though co-dependent experiences, we have divided the text into two parts:

Part I offers suggestions for embarking on the personal growth experience and success.

Part II pertains to meeting your soul mate and preparing you for marriage.

Having explored the process of making peace with your past experiences and hurts, attaining self-awareness and integration, you will be ready to begin your search and uplift your life with your soul mate, ensuring that after cleansing yourself of all past negativity, you do not allow your conscious mind to retrogress.

We offer a comprehensive plan on how to meet your soul mate and later collaborate on wedding and honeymoon plans and living arrangements. We also provide suggestions for managing your finances as a couple, family planning, and establishing open lines of communication to create a fulfilling, happy, prosperous, and successful married life.

Personal Success & Happiness

PART I

How to Achieve Personal Success and Happiness

Unchain yourself from the shackles of your past that prevent you from shining in the light of your highest potential.

CHAPTER 1

CLEANSING YOUR PAST, EMBRACING A NEW BEGINNING, AND PREPARING FOR A GREAT FUTURE

(A) *Taking a Good Look at Yourself*

To experience personal growth, you must first take an honest look at yourself from the inside and transport your thoughts into the past. Once you embark on that journey, you will learn from your mistakes and the pain that others have caused in your life. Understand that you may have carried this hurt inside you for a long time, and it may have been holding you back from the peace of mind, blessings, and prosperity that you deserve. Then, you can move forward into your life's purpose and mission.

Before venturing on that journey, you must situate yourself in a quiet place where you will not be interrupted. Shut down your telephone and let your thoughts and spirit transport you back to your first memories of your childhood—as far back as you can remember. (Your present age does not matter.) It is never too early or late to start your journey into a life of success, love, happiness, and abundance.

We call this exercise "cleansing your past." The process is simple and can only be done by you alone. You do not have to engage in any extravagant rituals or practices.

Although we realize that as you perform this exercise, you risk reliving painful experiences and sorrows. However, if you look at your past as an objective observer—as if you were objectively observing the movie of your own life story—you will be encouraged to revisit those circumstances—and the people—that caused your distress. Revisit the experience and find ways to forgive and cleanse your mind, heart, and spirit from those painful events.

If you find that you cannot attain the freedom you seek on your first attempt, keep trying! Do not jump to the next level until you feel entirely unburdened. Claim that sense of freedom! Mistakes and past hurts are like anchors tied to your limbs. This exercise is designed to unchain yourself from the shackles of your past that prevent you from shining in the light of your highest potential.

All of us have endured trying and difficult experiences, irrespective of race, culture, national origin, or socioeconomic status. We carry scars revealing the effects of such negativity on our bodies or in our thoughts. In one way or another, each one of us has been demoralized, belittled, or experienced discrimination in some form. Self-pity is not a solution to any of these roadblocks. It only keeps you from accessing your highest self. 'Pity parties' sometimes delude others into thinking that they are 'superior' or 'better,' and they place restrictions on your innate, limitless abilities. The concept of separation is an illusion. Everyone is on an equal playing field, all striving for the same essential building blocks of life: happiness, prosperity, success, abundance, and fulfillment. You will achieve such a balance when you complete your cleansing process and experience freedom from the painful experiences of your past.

As you watch the "movie of your past," write down all your negative experiences and lingering resentments on paper. Make sure that you write *everything* down without omitting a single memory. In the process, keep in mind that when you put pen to paper, your painful mistakes and transgressions have been eradicated.

After you complete your writing task, fold the paper in half and place it in a bag, along with two rocks and either drown it in the nearest body of water, burn or tear it so that it no longer exists. Instead of nursing your scars and giving weight to the negativity, you can attain blessings, achieve victory, and receive your spiritual medal of freedom, like a soldier returning home from the front lines of war. Life on earth is a battleground between the flesh and the spirit, and all of us must rise to the occasion and claim our victory with God's guiding hand.

The suggested exercise may seem to be "easier said than done." Still, when performed with sincerity and an open mind, happiness and success are foregone conclusions (as the readers of our "TLC" series have witnessed).

(B) *Establishing a Personal Relationship with The Creator*

To establish a personal relationship with God, you must acknowledge God's presence in every living being—everywhere in this universe. You just have to be willing to seek it out and recognize that the divine is ever-present in mind and spirit. No matter how you perceive God, the Creator is part of us and within us. The Master of the Universe is so all-encompassing that a gender designation for God is unnecessary. Most people think of the Almighty as a man with a long beard in a flowing gown, seated on a cloud, presiding over the earth, moon, stars, and all the planets and galaxies. Those who hold onto that perception try to make God into an entity that they can understand—within the limited scope of human understanding to feel closer to the divine.

However, shaping God to fit our definitions diminishes the Creator's infinite nature and the depth to which the divine presence encompasses everything. We relate to that presence when we acknowledge its supreme existence and take joy in that understanding. Challenging ideas of what God looks like or which belief system is 'right' or 'wrong' drives us away from the true essence of who the Supreme Architect is.

So, how do we establish a personal connection to God? Our relationship with the Almighty develops when we appreciate everything within our five senses. At the same time, we must recognize the existence of the infinite—the no-beginning-and-no-end quality of everything.

The process of acknowledging the infinite can be overwhelming, and we might feel small in the process, but that is okay. All things—even the small and seemingly insignificant—are components of *all.* In other words, everything is a reflection of God, and through the Almighty, we connect to each other. Therefore, how can we discriminate or hold each other in contempt when each one of us is a manifestation of God, the same Source that created all of us?

With this understanding, we can be in harmony, demonstrate love, kindness, acceptance, and reflect the face of God through good deeds and actions that serve others without having to search for a definition or assign the Almighty a gender or appearance. God is everything and is everywhere, personal to each of us in unique ways. The Almighty appears to us in every act of love that we bestow and receive, every word of encouragement, every beautiful form in nature, and in the hearts of our loved ones, friends, and all those who connect in genuine solidarity.

After you cleanse your mind, body, and spirit of past toxicity, you will be ready to embark on the journey toward lasting prosperity, happiness, success, and abundance fortified and directed by God's compass (or as we like to say, "GPS'"—"God's Personal Service"), to which you have a direct line.

Releasing your past allows you to embrace the present and look to the future with courage and optimism.

No matter what the weather brings or how many chores we must do, our attitude of gratitude will bring happiness and love to everyone we meet during the day.

CHAPTER 2

BEGINNING EACH DAY WITH AN ATTITUDE OF GRATITUDE

(A) *Expressing Your Gratitude*

Gratitude is one of the most powerful expressions in our lives and the lives of our family and friends. Appreciation also especially demonstrates our awareness of all the blessings in our lives. When we speak words of gratitude, we acknowledge our lives are filled with many blessings. The fact that we awaken each morning is, in and of itself, a gift of the present.

When we awake each day, we must express our gratitude—irrespective of whether we are in good physical health, in possession of our faculties, and with loved ones at our side. When we do so, we are ready to receive good health, abundance, happiness, and peace. Most of us experience more abundance than we can hope for, but arrogance sometimes prevents us from acknowledging the divine's presence and involvement. Each day brings different challenges, so we must never take one moment for granted.

Therefore, let us start each day with an attitude of gratitude. No matter what the weather brings or how many chores we must do, our attitude of gratitude will radiate happiness and cheer to everyone that we meet during the day.

(B) *There is a Purpose In All Challenges*

It is essential to acknowledge that life presents many tests and challenges that we must confront each day. That is why we are alive— to rise and respond to the challenges of each day. Everything that happens to us has a purpose and a reason. By expressing and practicing gratitude, we will be ready to experience our innate spiritual power.

Challenges or turns in the road are not necessarily a loss of direction. Instead, they can be—and often are—building blocks for much-needed growth experiences. For that reason, what we want might not be what we need at any given point in our lives.

For example, some people might think that having material wealth is all they need to make them happy. They believe that having that new car or house will be their pinnacle of success and joy. If they don't receive what they want, they somehow feel deprived. To be happy, you must transform the feeling of deprivation into a sense of empowerment, move through the challenge at hand, and learn from it. When you pass that test of resilience, the victory is much sweeter. So, suppose you want a new car or home. In that case, some event must precede your desired goal (e.g., the right job opportunity, a salary increase, involving the need for dedication to a specific discipline or career). Once we prove ourselves in that field of endeavor, we receive the blessings that we desire. In other words, a change from within has to occur before your outer circumstances conform to your wishes.

(C) *Following "GPS"*

To get what we seek most, we must relinquish our tight hold on the reigns and instead allow "GPS" ("God's Personal Service") to guide us on the path to our destination. In doing so, we acknowledge that what we strive to achieve is not the ultimate reason for our success. Rather, our success and happiness manifest our surrender and faith.

Most people know the famous song, "My Way," sung by Frank Sinatra, which expresses self-reliance and independence. When we stop trying to control our lives and focus on what we need instead of what we want, we are doing things "God's Way." (The song is one of our favorites to sing at Karaoke. Mordechai always replaces the words, "I did it my way" with "I did it God's way." Some people in the audience laugh, while others understand the message that he is trying to convey.

Refer to ***The Gratitude Prayer*** at the back of this book (page 123).

(D) *Helpful Practices*

To achieve personal growth and development, consider adhering to these practices:

- When you have questions or doubts, listen for answers in the whispers of your inner voice;
- Ask for forgiveness. If you make a mistake, repent and correct it;
- If something does not bring you inner peace, refrain from doing it;
- Love and respect yourself and everyone around you;
- Show love and kindness in everything you do;
- Be persistent and steadfast in every undertaking;
- Follow your dreams;
- Learn how to say "no" to things that are wrong for you and others;
- Take care of your body;
- Seek out those things that are in your best interests;
- If something goes wrong, believe that the event or circumstance had a purpose in facilitating your personal growth. You may not understand the reason immediately, but it will be revealed in time. Look for the message and the opportunity to learn from your challenges. Sometimes, shared pain heals wounds. Reach out and allow yourself to assist and be helped, in turn.

- Never give up, no matter how difficult the circumstances are;

- Trust that God is going to grant you victories;

- Say "Amen" when you hear someone affirming something positive or an inspirational prayer. There is a sense of holiness in that word that is meaningful to all who hear it. Believe that it will come to pass. When we say "Amen," both the giver and the receiver reap the benefits.

(E) *Reaching Out to Others*

One of the most profound ways of expressing gratitude is acknowledging others' attributes and efforts to create a better, more harmonious world through acts of lovingkindness. Consider the following examples:

(F) *The Two-Dollar Certificate*

In keeping with our personal mission to perpetuate acts of kindness, we give out a two-dollar bill to anyone whom God places in our path, whose kindness and love are worthy of acknowledgment in the form of a "Certificate of Recognition of Acts of Love and Kindness." When people receive our gesture, they are encouraged and inspired to continue the trend of spreading love and joy to others—not just because they receive the two-dollar certificate. The act of giving, in and of itself, signifies their gratitude to God. Even a small gesture of goodwill demonstrates that goodness and hope.

The Hebrew word "**Nata**n," meaning "to give," is a palindrome — it reads the same backward and forward, from right to left and vice versa. A friend of ours once pointed out that "each time you give with honorable intention, you receive much more because you are doing God's will."

Spreading love and goodness through gifts of the heart has a domino and cyclical effect that lasts not only in our temporal realm but throughout time into eternity.

(G) The "AY-YA-YA-YA-YAI!" Cheer

Another symbolic representation of gratitude that we adopted after a trip to Israel is the "AY- YA- YA- YA- YAI" cheer. In a gesture of appreciation for anyone—family members, friends, or others whom God inspires us to cheer in the Creator's name, we repeat that individual's name three times and then shout, "AY- YA- YA- YA- YAI!" As we cheer, we move our hands in the air, from one side to the other, and finally pour out blessings to the person with that motion, signifying that we are sprinkling goodness and prosperity upon them. This example does not require any monetary investment. You just have to be willing to seek out opportunities to pour blessings upon others from the heart.

Gratitude frees the heart and soul so that you can become part of an instrument of kindness, love, and peace to everyone you encounter.

Practice Daily Gratitude

We can be lights in the world through a tiny act,
one heartbeat at a time.

CHAPTER 3

COMMITTING TO DAILY READING OF POSITIVE AND MOTIVATIONAL MATERIAL

Upbeat, inspirational reading material reinforces the messages that we must learn in the School of Life. If we are diligent students, we might even earn a Ph.D. along the way. Positive messages are not expressions that we take in and then quickly disregard. Instead, we must integrate them into our daily life experiences.

When choosing to read inspirational words, pay attention to the writers' style and voice and what they are trying to convey. Does the message resonate with you, or is it 'going in one ear and out the other?' If the latter is true, immediately select another source of literature.

The reading can either be spiritual, religious, or secular. As long as it teaches you something, makes you think, and motivates you, you are in the correct zone.

Consider the following anecdotes and see what you derive from them. Take your time and read thoroughly. Then, write or type out your feelings and the lessons you have learned as you apply the messages to your own life.

(A) *Relativity*

This story is an old fable, but its timeless lesson encourages you to see the world from a different angle.

A farmer went to his trusted advisor and said, "I don't know what to do. There is so much noise in my house that it is driving me to distraction. The children are screaming; my wife is trying to calm them down; my neighbors call at all hours of the day. I'm at my wit's end."

"Try this," replied the wise advisor. "Go out into the fields, and take in one sheep, then bring in a cow. Come back tomorrow and let me know how things have changed."

The next day, the farmer returns and declares, "I'm still in a lot of distress. The noise is continuing, day and night. Now, I have the sheep and the cow singing to me 24/7. I know you meant well, but this was a bad idea."

"Just listen to me and continue to bring in an animal from your farm into your house daily. Return to me in a week," the advisor insisted.

A week passes, and the farmer follows his advisor's instructions.

"Now, things are intolerable at home. I have pigs, goats, chickens, and all kinds of animals in my house, along with my wife and children. I am miserable, and I have to say, so is my family. I have no idea what I'm going to do now."

"Well, just listen to me," the advisor said, undisturbed. "Take each animal, one by one, back to the fields. Return in a week, and let me know how things are going."

The farmer shook his head in disbelief. "My trusted advisor has gone mad," he whispered to himself.

Despite his skepticism, the farmer proceeded to follow instructions, taking each animal back to the fields. The following week, he returned to visit his advisor.

"So, tell me. How is everything with you?" the advisor wanted to know.

"You are a genius!" Exclaimed the farmer. "I did as you suggested and took all my animals back, and now, I'm so relieved. All I can hear are my children's screams, the sound of my wife's voice trying to calm them down, and the neighbors' calls. It's paradise!"

(B) *Troubles In the River*

Elizabeth Gilbert's account of her memorable experience on a New York City bus during rush hour.

It was a rainy, snowy winter's day, and people were expressing their frustration about the traffic, the weather, and other burdens. Observing his passengers' state of unrest, the bus driver got on the intercom and announced. While he could do nothing about the weather or the traffic, he suggested that each passenger "drop" their problems into the palm of his hand as they exited their stop. Then, on his route past the Hudson River, he would open the window and throw their troubles into the water.

Instantly, the somber mood on the bus turned into smiling faces and laughter, and the passengers who had once ignored each other suddenly became engaged in conversation. This was not a joke. The driver was intensely serious.

One by one, the exiting commuters placed their hands just above the driver's open palm and symbolically released their troubles into his hand. Some smiled as they did so, others were moved to tears, but everyone did as he had suggested.

Gilbert points out that we are all links in the chain of life—a life sometimes enshrouded in darkness, fear, and doubt. But each one of us, as individuals, can be a positive influence on those whose lives we touch—even strangers—by projecting kindness and love onto everyone we encounter. That is how we become lights in the world through a tiny act, one person at a time.

(C) *Affirmation—Albert Camus, French Philosopher/Author (1913-1960)*

In the midst of hate, I found there was, within me, an invincible love. In the midst of tears, I found there was, within me, an invincible smile. In the midst of chaos, I found there was, within me, an invincible calm.

I realized, through it all, that…
In the midst of winter, I found there was, within me, an invincible summer.

And that makes me happy. For it says that no matter how hard the world pushes against me, within me, there's something stronger — something better — pushing right back.

Motivational literature makes you think. Perhaps you can create your own. What have you read or learned today?

The burdens and challenges often faced by the human species are made lighter by words of wisdom.

May the Light Always Shine Within

Always follow your inner voice and have no fear in following its command.

CHAPTER 4

BELIEVE IN YOURSELF

(A) *Get to Know Yourself Better*

Each of us is born with innate potential encoded in our DNA from birth, and we are endowed with limitless abilities to achieve our mission on Planet Earth.

When you are born, part of your birthright and job is to understand the nature and extent of that potential and go for it! Did you ever see a baby examining its hands as if those limbs were the most miraculous things in the world? They *are*—because they are the seeds of potential to do whatever that child intends. Those hands can create, heal, invent, write, and perform millions of other tasks. When a child examines his hands, he acknowledges that he is beginning to know himself and understand the miracle of life.

As the child grows, he comes to recognize the miracles and signs of potential implanted in his mind, heart, and spirit—but knowing is not enough. He must then take steps in furtherance of that understanding and become his highest self.

(B) *Act In Furtherance of Your Potential*

An essential phase in your growth and development is taking that step in the direction of your dreams—the goals that you know you can attain—in the depth of your heart. How do you know? Your inner voice speaks to you. Sometimes, you get caught up in brain chatter when that voice calls to you from your soul, telling you which direction to take; always listen to your inner voice and have no fear in following through on its command.

When you ignore the 'inner voice,' you run the risk of losing your way, and your detour takes you in the opposite direction of your purpose. What you expect to hear from that voice and what you really hear are often very different. For example, while listening to your brain-static, you may believe that you are destined for a specific destination, and without pausing to acknowledge the whispers, you're turned around in the wrong direction. "I'm supposed to be X because that's what my relatives and friends say. But I really want to be Y because it's in my heart and mind to do that." What's in your heart and soul is the actual reality. No one can define or label you or determine your destiny.

(C) *Be the Co-Creator of Your Destiny*

When you follow the "inner whispers," you become the co-creator of your life, together with The Creator. The divine is your project manager, directing you at all times. You never have to be concerned or entertain doubt because you have a direct line to the Ultimate Source. Through prayer and acknowledgment, the Creator hears and sees all your intentions and is your steadfast ally. The Creator infused the Divine into you the day you were born and became part of your soul.

(D) *Do Not Be Afraid of Mistakes and Failure*

People often say that there isn't any room for mistakes, but your errors are blessings in disguise that fortify you to make more enlightened decisions going forward. Therefore, your self-belief must be inspired and enhanced in the face of failure, not diminished. Every misstep is a test on life's road to encourage you to improve yourself, be brave, and believe in yourself and your purpose. In other words, sometimes mistakes and failures are part of the process to pave the way for lasting achievements and successes. Get rid of those thoughts that diminish your self-worth as quickly as possible, and do not allow them to hold you back.

(E) *Avoid the Naysayers*

As you travel along the path toward attaining your purpose, there will always be naysayers who threaten to disrupt your joy and dreams. These individuals are often loud, controlling, and annoying, and they do not bear goodwill. Avoid them at all costs! Try to laugh in the face of their negativity and let their voices drown amid their own noise. Allow them their space as you go on your way—in a completely different direction. Naysayers are common elements that we confront every day to confirm our faith and determination to succeed. Be strong, firm and let yourself be guided by "GPS."

(F) *Claim Your Purpose, Accept Challenges and Look For Possibilities*

Once you discover your objective, proceed toward it, and arrive, claim your purpose. It's yours, and no one can take it from you. Accept it as your divine birthright and move through it like the expert you are. Do not deny yourself the blessings that the Creator has prepared for you.

Along the way, you will encounter unexpected hurdles, and you may even stumble. These setbacks are part of the journey. Remember that you are not alone. Be self-reflective, pray, and understand the lessons learned. Then, move ahead with an enhanced understanding of the circumstances and a commitment to greater possibilities beyond your wildest dreams. Because your potential is limitless, you must leave the door open to possibilities, rejoice in them, and handle them with confidence and humility.

(G) *The Differences Between Self-Belief and Arrogance*

People sometimes confuse the meaning of self-belief and arrogance. Self-belief is humble confidence, understanding who you are, what you can do, and where you are going in life. That confidence signifies your unity with your inner voice. By paying heed to it, you demonstrate your willingness to be a co-creator on the journey toward your purpose.

By contrast, arrogance is the false claim of 'superiority' over others, the unfounded belief that you are better than others in some fashion. Living in this false reality inevitably leads to the person's downfall.

Refer to the prayer *God Created You To Be,* located at the back of this book and inspirational lyrics at

www.makelifeasuccess.com

Listen to the inner whispers, believe in yourself, and proceed confidently in the direction of your dreams.

Thoughts, speech, and action determine outcomes in your life.

CHAPTER 5

UNDERSTANDING THE LAW OF ATTRACTION

What you think, how you communicate, and how you act will determine your quality of life and the daily events that shape it. The orchestral music of the universe accompanies you on your journey. Every aspect of the Grand Scheme is equal to the whole. So, whatever you think and do goes 'out there' into the universe. Thoughts, speech, and action determine outcomes in your life.

There are four essential components of the Law of Attraction:

(A) Your Thoughts and Visions
(B) Communication
(C) Initiative and Action
(D) Your Outcome

(A) *Your Thoughts and Your Visions:*

Your thoughts are the most powerful magnets that attract everything in creation. Even when you are unaware of it, your mind processes countless thoughts—the forces that create our present and future for better or worse. Who you are now, what you possess, what you are going through are the products of every thought you have had in the past and entertain in the present.

With that awareness, the question becomes, ***how do you know whether you're thinking positive or negative thoughts?***

The answer is simple. Each one of us has a barometer in us, comprised of *feelings* that you can monitor. If you are happy, loving, friendly, and energetic, your thoughts are focused on goodness, love, abundance, hope, and happiness.

On the other hand, if you feel depressed, lack enthusiasm, are weary and unwilling to socialize, go to work or school, you have been harvesting the wrong thoughts.

What can you do to transform negative influences into positive energy? When watching TV or listening to the radio, you can switch the channel or station to benefit your state of mind and needs. The same is true with the Law of Attraction. You are the master of your life. Monitor and check your feeling-barometer to determine whether you want to change the channel or station. In other words, become a detective who evaluates the individuals in your environment—your family, friends, students, traveling companions, co-workers, etc. If they speak negatively about everything (including the weather), gossip, or are generally dissatisfied with life, they sap all the positive energy out of your environment and carry a ball and chain around with them. To the extent possible, avoid those individuals. Instead, surround yourself with people that compliment you, encourage your goals, endorse your beliefs, and are fun to be around. Along the way, you will observe the difference between those who are energy-enforcers and those who are energy-extractors.

God allows you to surround yourself with both types of people to help you develop your feeling-barometers.

(B) *Communication—The Way You Articulate Your Thoughts*

Thoughts become words. When you speak something into existence, whether it is good or bad, you articulate your desires and project your wishes into the universe. God will allow you to orchestrate the outcome you desire, whether it is good or bad. That declaration helps to solidify your intentions and makes them come to life immediately. Therefore, you must replace negative with positive thoughts. Never speak negative thoughts into existence as they might take you on an undesirable, misguided path.

To help yourself to change your channel from negativity to positivity, you can perform the following simple exercise:

Write down your positive thoughts and desires on paper, on your cell phone, or computer. Do not concentrate on how they are going to happen. Allow the Law of Attraction to provide you with the answers, and you will receive blessings in your best interests. Print them out or have them accessible. Read those ideas aloud to yourself every day, every week, or as many times as possible, share them with a loved one or confidant— only those who feed into your positivity. Do not share them with people who complain or dwell in the negative. If, by chance, people put a dent in your thoughts, just press the 'delete' button in your mind—as you would on an electric device and walk away from the negative influences. Understand that your desires and wishes are not concepts but real and present realities as well as future prospects.

(C) *Initiative and Action*

Once you understand the power of your thoughts, you are ready to act as a co-creator of your destiny. Your dreams remain on hold until you decide to take action. Some people say that the cemetery is filled with the most fantastic inventions and ideas that forever will remain unfulfilled because no one put them into effect.

Where do you want to be in five or ten years? Create a life plan on paper as if you were the producer of your own film or writing a book. Continue to add to it as you grow and change them. Revisit them as you evolve in mind and spirit and see how many of the things you envisioned have come to pass. That will give you confidence and affirm that the Law of Attraction is real and effective. The same will be true of your life plan.

Each time you change the plan, read it aloud to yourself or someone you trust. Declare it as if it is already occurring or within your reach—because it is happening! What you focus on will expand and materialize.

A writer, movie producer, or anyone who has an idea but never acts on developing their creative ideas misses out on the golden opportunity to act upon all of the possible choices that are before them.

The Frog Anecdote:

A grandfather wanted to teach his grandson about the importance of acting upon beliefs and desires. So, he told his grandson the following story.

"Once, five frogs were resting on a log floating on a lake. It was a beautiful day, and the temperature was ideal. Three of the frogs thought about jumping into the lake for the longest time, but the other two were indecisive.

As time passed, how many frogs jumped into the lake? Take a guess!" The grandfather urged the grandson.

The grandson responded with confidence. "Of course, the three frogs that thought about jumping."

The grandfather replied, "Sorry! None of the frogs jumped. You see, they only thought about jumping in without following through."

The story's moral: Only by taking action can you achieve your objective.

You must take the potential energy and translate it into power in motion ("kinetic energy"). That catalyst makes the wheels turn—not only in your mind but in physical reality. In doing so, you are acting in collaboration with God, guided by the Almighty's GPS, 'doing it God's way' and following through on your desired goal.

(D) *Your Outcome*

After you have performed the groundwork for achieving your goals, you're ready for the fun part: watching your vision take shape, and you may be surprised by the changes that unfold. Be part of the process and objectively observe what happens to you. Monitor your thoughts and choose your words carefully. Try to avoid using negative expressions commonly spoken in everyday conversation. Words can be immensely powerful once they are communicated, but they can also damage your future, especially if you repeat negative phrases and expect different results. It is easier to erase your thoughts and not produce harmful effects than to erase spoken words.

Once words get 'out there,' the universe and everyone around you hear them, and what you want will materialize. And if you have a family, be careful what you say to your children. They retain everything, and negative words will impact their future.

In all things, make sure that you remain true to your personal goals. Even if your dreams take longer to manifest than you initially expected, you are still on your way.

At times, before you receive the fruits of the Law of Attraction, you may have to go through a few extra steps (life lessons). These apparent detours will enhance your faith in your ability to achieve your objectives.

Most of all, enjoy the ride and appreciate the scenery! Life is beautiful, and when you are confronted with detours, the universe shows you other possibilities that could improve your decision-making process and your life.

Think, envision, speak, and take action to accomplish your dreams. God always rewards the dreamer, the communicator, and the doer.

Love

If you sense someone you know and love requires your understanding, time, or help, offer it freely. Don't hold back.

CHAPTER 6

TREASURING FAMILY AND OTHERS WITH UNIVERSAL LOVE (AGAPE)

Treasuring family and others alike is an essential component of quality of life. Without interacting with people around us, life loses its joy and meaning. The path you travel leads you to encounter and learn, provide comfort and be as one, in joyful solidarity, with others.

(A) *Compassion, Kindness, Respect, and Love Toward Others*

We define compassion as "feeling with someone" with a profound sense of understanding, heart, and soul. The word and the deeds that accompany it require a willingness to open oneself up to the problems and suffering of others, listen, or lend a helping hand. Doing so leads to the realization that we are all connected in lasting ways.

We develop compassion as we navigate the School of Life. It's up to us to choose to engage in acts of compassion. We have one lifetime in which to make a positive impact on the lives we touch. Even if we perform one act of kindness in a day, the effect of that exchange mutually benefits all parties involved for all time.

Demonstrating loving-kindness for family and others should be as natural as breathing. Parents, children, spouses, grandparents, extended family, and others should be in continuous harmony. Such a state of being is sometimes difficult to maintain, but you can achieve it through time, consistent practice, and determination.

A unified Circle of Love and Life enables you to have a healthy approach to living an optimistic worldview. Everyone in your immediate space—even those you don't know—holds a special place in the tapestry of creation and the legacies they carry. The best and purest demonstration of compassion is to honor them in the same way you recognize your own self-worth. When you practice tolerance and acceptance of others, you enhance that feeling toward yourself and grow in kindness and love. Selfishness is an inherent trait in all of us, but the most effective way to control it is by practicing the art of compassion toward yourself and others.

If you sense someone you know and love requires your understanding, time or help, offer it freely. Don't hold back. Respect the sensitivity of the moment, and let the person know that you are there, even just to listen or be there for them. Proceed gently and humbly. Ask what they want or need and show that you are willing to "step up to the plate" whenever they call on you.

Feel free to share the suggestions that you have derived from this book. In doing so, you will put your knowledge into practice for the benefit of others. That is compassion in action. Treasure those times and the chance to make a difference in the lives of others.

In the case of friends, co-workers, and strangers, you can offer different levels of intervention. Depending upon how close you are to a person, you should tread cautiously in providing advice. In other words, know your boundaries. If you have established yourself as a confidant, you can speak and act more freely. On the other hand, if you have a professional relationship, respectfully seek permission to offer an opinion rather than imposing your views on others.

If a stranger in need crosses your path, be open to offering help if doing so is within your capacity. Take care to keep your eyes open to every possible scenario. Unfortunately, not everyone has the best of intentions. Simply ask whether you can do anything to improve their circumstances. In doing so, you demonstrate agape or universal love for that person. You don't have to know someone to feel and show that love. In sharing the same space, everyone must look out for one another. For example, if you see a sight-impaired person walking across the street and that individual cannot see the light changing, you may want to offer that helpful information. If someone loses a personal item, return it to them if you find it. If you see someone in physical danger, seek help, or if you can do so safely, offer assistance.

(B) *Demonstrate the Above Without Judgment*

We are here to love, not to judge. All of us in this life go through tests and tribulations to purify our souls and elevate our spirits. We have a responsibility to help one another, and by doing so, we grow and obtain greater wisdom. You never know if the opportunity to help someone will benefit you in the long run. No one is immune to trials and tribulations. If COVID-19 taught us anything, it is that we are all susceptible to forces entirely beyond our control. The pandemic has taught us to take time and appreciate everyone around us and savor the moments of togetherness and mutual appreciation for each other. The only one you are allowed to judge is yourself; the rest is in God's hands.

When we respect and love others, we become 'decorated' soldiers in the School of Life.

No dream is ever too big—the bigger the dream, the more exciting its manifestation.

CHAPTER 7

~※~

CREATE A 'BUCKET LIST'— DREAM BIG!

(A) *Origin of the Term "Bucket List"*

Creating a bucket list means setting out a list of things you most want to achieve before departing the earth. The term originated in the 2007 film, *The Bucket List*, with Jack Nicholson and Morgan Freeman.[1] The two main characters, terminally ill men, set off on an adventure to accomplish their hopes and dreams before they died.

(B) *Creating Your Bucket List*

While the bucket list is a tool for envisioning your goals before you complete your earthly journey, anyone can write one—with light years ahead of them! Celebrate life! You can call it your 'Someday List' or assign it any name that serves its true purpose. Don't think of it as a prelude to 'kicking the bucket.' Instead, live each day, rejoice in the wonders of the world, and expect that with the passing

---

[1] Zimmer, B. (2015, May 29). The Origins of 'Bucket List' Retrieved March 13, 2021, from https://www.wsj.com/articles/the-origins-of-bucket-list-1432909572

of each day, you move closer to accomplishing your list's objectives.

Take the list seriously. Think about all the things that would make you and your family happy and help you accomplish your life's mission. Don't dwell on the negative and avoid thoughts that tend to negate the fulfillment of your list, such as "We don't have enough money" or "I can't find the time." Claim what you want to achieve as yours before it happens—much like the vision board discussed in Chapter 4. Remember that your thoughts, actions, written and spoken expressions take shape in the universe as desires and wishes. God will make them manifest as long as they are in your best interest.

(C) *Dream Big!*

Your bucket list is attainable no matter your circumstances in life. Because you are a precious creation, you are limitless—just by being alive. The world is yours for the asking, shared, and enjoyed by every living being.

No dream is ever too big—the bigger the dream, the more exciting its manifestation. Think back to when you were a child. Each day, your parents might have measured your growth by telling you to stand against a wall. They marked your height, and over time, the mark moved further from the ground. Or think of the money that you placed in the bank when you opened your very first account. The more money you put in, the more it grew, day by day.

The same is true of your dreams. To 'grow' them, you must allow for the passage of time—on God's watch—coupled with your investment, which can either be in the form of physical action, monetary contributions, or concerted planning and organization. Your dream may take time to flourish, but the longer it takes to actualize, the sweeter the victory will be.

Whether you seek an education, professional career, social advancement, or a lasting relationship with your soul mate, your goals are as close to realization as your thoughts. See yourself getting that promotion, that stellar academic GPA, or your ideal soul mate. If you can dream, you can attain whatever your heart desires. Persistence and belief are essential to realizing the goals in your written list, and with each passing day, you will move closer to your dream's fulfillment.

Along the way, you may encounter stumbling blocks, but never give up. Allow yourself to learn from the fumbles. Then dust yourself off and move forward with confidence.

(D) *Live Each Day In Expectation of Your Dreams*

Once you go through the effort of investing physically, emotionally, and financially in your dream, go for it! Don't allow doubt or fear to set in, and don't deny yourself or your loved ones the joy of its fulfillment. You earned it—just because you're *you*. Reap the reward, humbly and with self-assurance, and lastly (but perhaps most significantly), share the abundance and prosperity with loved ones and friends. No experience has profound meaning unless you reach the top holding the hands of those most important in your life.

As you accomplish your objectives, seize the opportunity to share your good fortune with others. Express and demonstrate the Creator's blessings that have graced your life and encourage others to seek and attain their highest potential—just as you have—perhaps even to a greater extent. Shared joys increase the prosperity of others and the universe as a whole.

Dreaming and living your goals is the essence of a joyful existence.

PART II

MEETING YOUR SOUL MATE AND PREPARING FOR YOUR MARRIAGE

52 •

Preliminary Observations

Connecting with your essence and knowing yourself prepares you for the next step: finding your soul mate. First, however, it is important to understand the difference between male and female approaches.

Understanding the General Distinctions Between Male and Female Approaches

Although we, as human beings, have a fundamental need for love and the pursuit of happiness, males and females often adapt to circumstances differently. These distinctions are real and deeply rooted in human nature and physiology. The following generalizations apply to *some* individuals, depending on gender.

Males are natural hunter-gatherers and providers. They use their intuition to solve problems analytically and act on their 'hunches.' The male is often a bottom-liner who will not engage in such activities as shopping for extended periods. He will go to the store with a definitive objective, obtain the desired item, and leave.

The male generally does not freely express pain or emotions voluntarily and often conceals aspects of himself for fear of appearing weak or vulnerable.

The male is a risk-taker and invests his faith in a positive outcome. He is tough and resilient but requires reassurance and appreciation for his efforts and feels fulfilled knowing that his abilities positively affect those around him.

Females are child-bearers, nurturers, and givers, grounded in feelings as much as intellect. They are reflective, patient, and discerning. If a woman finds an item that she can purchase at a more affordable price, she will go the extra mile (quite literally) to obtain the discount.

Women are given to expressing themselves without restraint and welcoming the same quality in others. They demonstrate vulnerability more readily than men and do not feel shame or reservation in displaying their emotions.

In general, females enjoy reflecting instead of taking risks or leaps of faith. They ponder rather than act on impulse and often consider the repercussions of their actions—on themselves and others.

With regard to intimacy, males will sometimes view the consummation of love as an act, whereas women view it as a romantic experience. Each has a different viewpoint. The male has a direct approach, while the female likes to be pampered and prepare for such a beautiful and significant act. When the intimacy ends, the male usually wants to get up. On the other hand, the female prefers to stay for a while and reminisce about the wonderful time the couple had.

Therefore, we recommend that in recognition of the female's desire to be lavished with love, the male consider taking time to romanticize her prior to making love to enhance the overall experience of true romance.

We are aware that personalities vary depending upon genetics and environment. You might consider adding your qualifications to the list and see how they compare with our suggestions. It is always enlightening to acknowledge and celebrate differences and learn from each other.

The Heart Has Its Own Wisdom

Your soulmate is the essence you admire—similar to you but with your own characteristics and habits.
When soulmates meet, two hearts become one.

CHAPTER 1

THE DEFINITION OF "SOUL MATE" AND HOW TO USE THE LAW OF ATTRACTION TO FIND YOUR 'KINDRED SPIRIT'

Once you have developed a sense of who you are as an individual with a healthy dose of self-confidence, humility, gratitude, and a clear vision for your future, you possess the ability to move forward toward finding your soul mate.

(A) *The Definition of "Soul Mate"*

Your soul mate is the person you feel you have known all your life—the kindred spirit you can trust and with whom you can share your life's journey. When you are together, you experience not only the spark of romance—the racing of hearts and mutual physical 'chemistry'—but also ideological, emotional, and spiritual common ground. Your soul mate is the essence you admire—similar to you but with his or her own distinct characteristics and habits. This individual is your perfect partner in love and life, deserving of the highest recognition, words of praise, and devotion. But if this person exists in the world, how can we find each other? The answer is by using the Law of Attraction.

(B) *How to Use the Law of Attraction to Find Your 'Kindred Spirit.'*

(1) *Your Thoughts and Visions*

Although the basic concept of the Law of Attraction, when applied to finding your soul mate, is nearly identical to envisioning your individual goals and dreams, it operates slightly differently. This time, the object of your vision is your soul mate. Therefore, instead of imagining an action—seeing your desired goal as an end in itself—picture your perfect soul mate. We suggest creating a list of all the attributes and unique characteristics you seek in your projected love interest.

Begin the attribute list with "My soul mate will be," and fill in the blanks. Don't be shy to 'dream big' and dare to state your purpose—even if it is a 'pie-in-the-sky' objective, such as "My soul mate will be royalty." (That can signify more than a title; it can also mean nobility of spirit.) Remember: if you don't ask, the universe won't know what you want.

Then, see yourself in the presence of your soul mate. Feel the joy of meeting and getting to know that individual. And acknowledge the butterflies in your stomach when that happens. Hear that person's laughter, recognize their wit, and marvel at their words of admiration. You are in the moment; it's not an abstraction; it's yours to claim.

Bear in mind that sometimes the universe presents us with a different person than the one we envisioned. Always have an open mind, be willing to adapt, and take a chance by getting to know the individual entirely. The one you *need* will complete your life more readily than your ideal version of a soul mate.

(2) *Communication*

Once you have envisioned and claimed your vision of your ideal partner, you can express your goals for encountering that individual to others. Make inquiries among the people you know and trust and inform them that your heart is open to socializing and dating. Ask those within your circle of colleagues, either at work, school, or other places of interaction, to guide you to the right source of contact. People who know and respect you will work in your best interest.

We strongly suggest that you refrain from consulting and communicating with people you do not know or trust, such as those you randomly 'meet' on the Internet. The Web is an excellent resource for endless information, but you must use it wisely and discriminately. Many people falsely represent themselves. As a result, sometimes you may experience adverse effects. We encourage you to stay focused and follow your intuition.

Sometimes, it may help to read your attribute list aloud to yourself. By doing so, you call forth (speak into existence) the energy required to manifest your wish. Essentially, by hearing yourself say the words, you actualize the thought. Then, you must take steps to make it happen.

(3) *Initiation and Action*

Speaking words without action is like purchasing a car without a motor and wheels. You have the foundation, but the mechanisms must be in place to propel the vehicle forward. Besides communicating with people you trust, you must take the initiative to 'go after' your dream/soul mate.

How will you go about the process? *Where* will you go? Perhaps you will join an organization, go to a lecture series, social gathering, or congregate with friends in your house of worship. Wherever you go, the open door to your heart will lead you in the right direction. Remember to listen to your 'inner whispers' and follow through on what they teach you to do. When you least expect that your soul mate will appear, your significant other might materialize before your eyes. Have you ever heard of soul mates meeting in elevators or 'by coincidence' on the bus or the street? These scenarios are not just the stuff of a screenwriter's ideas. They happen all the time. When you free yourself from the artificial chains that bind (e.g., lack of self-confidence, a negative, can't-do attitude, or deliberately sabotaging yourself by saying that dreaded word, "never"), you experience limitless possibilities and surprises.

(4) *Your Outcome*

Your outcome is the result of persistently following and practicing # 1 through # 3 (above).

A wise person once said, "You cannot expect to receive different results if you continue doing the same things. "If you want to reap more beneficial outcomes, you must learn from the past, take the initiative, speak your dreams into reality, and envision that goal taking shape.

When you find your loved one, you attain success and happiness
by helping each other achieve your mission.

CHAPTER 2

ATTITUDES AND PRACTICES THAT FOSTER A HEALTHY RELATIONSHIP

The person you choose as your soul mate must physically, emotionally, intellectually, and spiritually appeal to you. When that happens, you must engage in soul-searching to discover whether God has destined that person to be in your life.

Below, we offer some of the most significant practices for a lasting rock-solid relationship with your soul mate.

(A) *Trust*

During the dating process, both parties experience excited anticipation of communicating and spending time together. The 'getting-to-know-you' phase is the foundation for marriage and all the responsibilities that go along with uniting your life. You must acknowledge the blessing of your union and identify with each other as soul mates. You came together through the power of physical attraction, and you must determine whether your individual makeup and mutual chemistry are right for each other. Once you do so, you will freely share your love and enjoy the happiness, prosperity, and blessings that lie ahead of you for many years on earth and into eternity.

Nevertheless, some couples who deeply love each other are unprepared for how marriage works and the pitfalls that cause it to fail. It is essential to know that intimacy is not the barometer of your future relationship. However, when combined with genuine love, it is a vital aspect of any soul mate connection. The most difficult challenges arise when one or both parties hide past experiences, conceal habits and vices, fail to disclose their beliefs, show a disinclination to discuss family issues and other topics that they guard or consider 'secret'. Therefore, an open dialogue is essential to establish mutual trust.

You do not need to like the same things, share the same belief systems, or hold identical opinions. Instead, your profound love enables you to establish a foundation of mutual understanding and trust so that you can help each other through life's challenges. When you decide to wed, both of you will express the following promise in your vows:"…in sickness and in health, for richer or poorer," into eternity. Couples recite this pledge in religious and secular ceremonies alike.

Trusting your soul mate, as in any other relationship, is your safety zone. It signifies your level of comfort in your soul mate's presence, knowing that whatever confidences you share or experiences you have together, the other person always has your back.

Trust is an essential ingredient to solidify your love, and you should commit to each other with an open heart. Jealousy, fear, and doubt are destructive to your happiness and violate the principles of trust. Always maintain open communication. Do not jump to conclusions or allow your mind to wander when disharmony strikes. Do not be influenced by current trends and behavioral practices, often witnessed in the media, that tend to undermine you or your soul mate's self-worth and confidence. Instead, remain alert to negative commentaries about you or your soul mate—even those that come from family members who mean well. Even when you believe that such statements do not affect you, your subconscious mind registers them; they manifest in your body language and generate feelings of mistrust that can potentially destroy your mutual feelings of trust and equilibrium.

(B) *Reputation*

You can tell that your soul mate is trustworthy when you discover that he or she has a good reputation in the community, your circle of mutual friends, or those you know individually. If your soul mate has a general reputation for being reliable, honest, forthright, and universally liked, you can safely conclude that investing your heart is a safe bet. On the other hand, if people who know your soul mate hesitate to endorse their trustworthiness, you must investigate whether the 'red flag' is valid. Sometimes, people spread rumors to hurt or undermine a person's credibility. Do not take everything at face value. The best tactic is to "trust but verify," as President Ronald Reagan said. Some people go to extremes and pull personal credit and criminal records to determine trustworthiness. But beware! Electronic reports are not foolproof. So, confront your soul mate and have an open-hearted dialogue about issues concerning both of you.

(C) *Reliability*

We have all heard the expression, "S/he is a fair-weather friend." Some people favor you or take an interest in you only when things are going well, but when stress, disappointments, or sorrows enter the picture, the individual takes off at lightning speed.

In finding out about your soul mate's reliability, ask about how that person reacts in different circumstances and if she/he is willing to offer comfort and help in times of need and cares about the family's and community's welfare. If they play sports, find out whether they are good teammates and keep their commitments to their team. If they are only there for you when the sun shines, have an open discussion and confront your soul mate with your discovery. Question them on the subject of commitment and how their conduct will translate into family life.

(D) *Supportiveness*

Not only must your soul mate care about you. Your chosen love interest must also promote your well-being and growth by benefitting each other with every action. The more a benefit results from their efforts on your behalf, the more you can trust them. Your soul mate must not only be there for you; they must work to promote your welfare in every aspect of your life. They must defend you and be your ally when gossip-loving naysayers threaten to disrupt your joy. Your soul mate need not agree with you on every topic or viewpoint. They only need to respect your perspectives and your right to express them.

One of the most critical aspects of supportiveness is the degree to which your soul mate demonstrates love and solidarity with family members. If your soul mate honors and cherishes their relatives, the chances are that they will mirror that behavior in your marriage. If either of you doesn't seem to demonstrate love and supportiveness, you should broach the subject and decide how to correct that deficiency within your family circle. Only then can you hope to move on with a healthy outlook.

(E) *Communication*

No relationship can endure without open communication. However, if your soul mate exhibits a good reputation, reliability, and supportiveness, communication will be the next most crucial building block for a good marriage. In other words, if the person you love will, indeed, become your soul mate, they must be respectful of your privacy and keep the communication channels open. If, on the other hand, you discover that a meaningful dialogue is not possible, you might have to look for ways to rectify the problem. Still, you will be better off knowing the truth earlier, confronting the issue, and resolving it, if possible. If you cannot resolve the matter, discuss how it will affect your relationship in general in the future.

Listen to your soul mate carefully so as not to misconstrue their words and intentions. When we properly receive honest, open disclosure, we demonstrate that we genuinely care and are willing to make the relationship work. It is important to receive the messages from the person directly and not from third parties. This reminds us of the game we used to play when we were children to demonstrate how messages are delivered and received from one person to another.

The Message Game

When we were young, we used to play a game with fifteen or twenty friends. We would form a circle. Then, from left to right, the first person would write a message on a piece of paper and whisper that exact message to the individual next to them. That person then had to pass on the *precise* message to the next and so on. Finally, the last person would take their turn and state the message aloud to the original presenter. Then when the last person would present the message and the first would read the original statement, we found that they differed entirely.

The game's purpose was twofold: (1) to determine each person's receptiveness to the original message, and (2) to observe how each person disclosed the message as passed from the initial presenter to the last. The more we played the game, the more we observed how drastically the message's meaning changed from the initial statement to the last.

Respect

Mutual respect is a vital aspect of every lasting relationship. Without that foundation, love is just a term of art or a mere physical attraction. There are four coexisting elements of respect: (1) tolerance/understanding, (2) awareness, (3) security, and (4) validation.

The Elements of Respect

(1) *Tolerance/Understanding*

To establish an enduring relationship, both parties must demonstrate tolerance and understanding without judgment. As we mentioned above, no two individuals think alike at all times. However, you can respect another person's right to believe and express their opinions freely without criticism, ridicule, or bullying (dominance).

Tolerance and understanding build confidence in your soul mate to speak without restraint, knowing that you will receive their words open-heartedly, agreeing to disagree amicably, or utilize the most powerful ingredient in a good relationship: *compromise.*

If your soul mate hesitates in speaking their mind, they cannot proclaim to love and trust you for fear of repercussions (e.g., rejection or the backlash of criticism).

(2) *Awareness*

Awareness signifies being alert to your soul mate's beliefs and opinions. Love your soul mate as a totality: their physical appearance, thoughts, actions and modes of expression. When you are aware, you are alive in their presence, anticipating what they will say or do in a given situation, and you demonstrate how much you love and accept each other just as you are. Your alertness to your soul mate's actions and reactions forges a bond between the two of you that no person or situation can sever. (For example, when two people finish each other's sentences, you can tell that they are either a couple or close relatives.) You are in sync, bound by mutual awareness of the other.

For over fifty-seven years, we have been blessed with an awareness of each others' needs and wants. Since the early years, we have anticipated each other's thoughts and expressions—even before uttering a word. However, some couples remain together for many years and resort to sarcastic or hurtful remarks that negate the concept of awareness. That kind of behavior is destructive to the marital relationship.

(3) *Security*

Respectfulness manifests in a sense of security with your soul mate. Knowing that you can 'be yourself' without the need to impress your soul mate or relatives establishes a unique comfort level between you. Your soul mate should fully appreciate you for who you are. Surprises are lovely, especially at the beginning of a relationship. But predictability has its benefits and is often underrated as uninteresting or mundane. Predictability provides a feeling of security (e.g., a kiss at the door when your soul mate returns home from work; a loving glance in a crowd of people, indicating "I love you;" an embrace when you say or do something thoughtful). Security is your seal of approval of each other.

(4) *Validation*

Like security, everyone requires validation—a verbal or physical expression of praise demonstrating that their life matters and has value. When you know that you are of importance to your soul mate, the world becomes your oyster. With your feet firmly planted on the ground, you can reach for the stars. You realize that no matter what you say or do, there is someone in the world who 'gets you.' Naturally, everyone has flaws, but to someone, you are the universe, and that person is the same to you. That feeling gives you a sense of invincibility. In this often uncertain world, that is one of life's greatest blessings.

The Relationship Between Love, Trust, and Respect

Love, trust, and mutual respect must go hand-in-hand if soul mates want to maintain and enhance their relationship for a long time and into eternity. Suppose you profess to love your soul mate without trusting and respecting them. In that case, the chances are that you're experiencing physical attraction without an underlying heart and soul connection and a sense of commitment. Therefore, commit to demonstrating mutual love, trust, and respect in all aspects of your lives together.

The Difference Between Behaviors of the Flesh and the Spirit

To have a successful and happy relationship, we must understand that each of us is born with natural behaviors and impulses that are integral parts of the flesh (e.g., greed, desire, selfishness, lust, fear, hate, etc.). But God infuses into each one of us the spirit that we need to fulfill our missions on earth. The spirit has the natural qualities of love, patience, faith, harmony, understanding, compromise, and peace (among other attributes).

Your spirit and flesh must operate in cooperation with each other to accomplish your earthly purpose. When you find your loved one, you attain success and happiness by helping each other to achieve your mission while you are living and into the next world. We suggest that you practice the approaches outlined in this text by relying on your spiritual attributes, not the impulses of the flesh. Before expressing yourself or acting impulsively, pass each thought, action, and expression through your spiritual funnel to determine the source of your idea or statement. When you deal with your soul mate and family, make sure, always, that the spirit serves as your guiding compass with love, patience, faith, harmony, understanding, peace, and compromise.

A successful love collaboration occurs when both parties agree to disagree and openly express their thoughts on various topics—especially where divergent opinions are concerned.

CHAPTER 3

THE IMPORTANCE OF COMPROMISE AND OPEN COMMUNICATION

It is no exaggeration to state that compromise is an essential element in any relationship—particularly regarding couples' interactions. When two people meet and fall in love, they are initially strangers coming into the relationship with different ideas, upbringings, and habits. A successful love collaboration occurs when both parties agree to disagree and openly express their thoughts on various topics—especially where divergent opinions are concerned. Issues involving opposite or distinct viewpoints arise in both the home and social spheres, and in some instances, when spouses work together.

It is important to note that sometimes, compromise involves a degree of sacrifice, but in reality, you do not give up anything at all. Instead, you forge a closer bond by contributing to the relationship in some way and maintaining stability and peace.

Below, we detail how compromise operates, always with love, open dialogues, and mutual understanding.

(1) Domestic Life

(A) *Chore Responsibilities*

Once couples commit to each other, they form a co-equal partnership, understanding that each must contribute to the relationship—and everything that goes along with it—for the benefit of both parties. Fortunately, we no longer live in an era in which men and women assume stereotypical roles. Although these are sometimes implicit (e.g., women assume domestic and nurturing responsibilities), such stereotypes have receded into the dustbin of history. Men play an integral part in their family's life and readily step in to assist in every aspect of homemaking and building. Day to day tasks, such as taking out the trash, washing dishes, housekeeping, and taking care of the children, belong to both the female and male figures in the relationship. Anyone who breaches their valued right to contribute to the well-being of the family unit must rethink their position and offer their intervention. Compromise is of the essence. If one party to the relationship does not feel up to par, the other must shoulder the responsibility on their behalf—willingly, with concern, and compassion. Also, an offer of assistance out of the clear blue sky will demonstrate to your soul mate that you genuinely care about them.

(B) *Compromise*

Everyone who enters a relationship brings different habits and family practices that are entirely foreign to both of you. These habits and practices may not be readily perceivable at first glance during the "Fantasy Phase." However, once you cohabitate, they come to the surface and sometimes surprise you. One partner might come from a family where expressing opinions is viewed as disrespectful. The other partner's family might interpret silence from the other person as a sign of disrespect. That can cause tension and frustration in the relationship. Therefore, the two of you need to make your own rules to determine how you will communicate *without* bringing your families' influences into the equation. In this way, you face situations head-on without confrontation.

For example, your soul mate may be accustomed to sleeping on one side of the bed or one of you may be used to making the bed in the morning. If both of you have the same-side preference, and if you are accustomed to awakening and leaving the bed unmade, challenges may arise—unless you arrive at a mutually beneficial arrangement. Honest, open communication and willingness to compromise are the best strategies. Remember that helping one another is natural and must not turn into argumentation and resentment. This type of discussion may sound trivial, but it can resolve a world of potential pitfalls in the relationship—not to mention sleepless nights.

At times, compromise is not enough, and a complete overhaul of habits becomes necessary. Suppose your soul mate has unfavorable habits (e.g., unhealthy dietary preferences or habits, such as smoking, drinking or behaving as if they were single). In that case, you may want to suggest that to have a happy relationship gently, they must refrain from these behaviors, focus on a long, lasting relationship. As with other routine engagement methods, such changes occur most effectively through loving, honest communication, understanding, and encouragement—never with an attitude of dominance or anger. All of us have traits that we must improve if we want to live a healthy and happy relationship.

(C) *The Significance of Honest Dialogue and Mutual Understanding*

The Spinach Pie Story

We have already emphasized the importance of communication between couples, but it cannot be overstated. Deficiencies in dialogue can lead not only to argumentation but also life-long misconceptions.

Perhaps no other story in our memory illustrates the essential nature of communication better than the true account of *The Spinach Pie* that one couple shared with us upon celebrating their 52nd wedding anniversary. When her husband approached her parents to ask for her hand in marriage, the woman told us that her mother baked a spinach pie and other specialties. The gentleman did not like spinach, but because he was on a mission to receive her parents' permission and blessings to marry their daughter, he ate the spinach pie with tremendous gusto. The mother watched the way he ate the spinach pie and gave him another piece . . . and then another . . . and he forced himself to eat it, saying that it was delicious.

After the couple got married, the wife cooked the spinach pie that her mother taught her to make at least once a week. When her husband came home, she would say, "Darling, I prepared your favorite dish that you enjoyed so much at my mother's house when you proposed to me. Silently, he would say to himself, here we go again! I must force myself to eat the spinach pie that I hate so much. For fifty years, the husband kept his secret, but when the couple celebrated their 50th anniversary, he decided not to eat any more spinach pie. He said to her, "darling, I must confess something that I have been keeping from you for the longest time.

She listened carefully with a confused expression on her face, thinking that her husband was about to reveal something very serious. Instead, he said, "I hate spinach, and I cannot eat any more spinach pie or anything cooked with spinach,

"I HATE SPINACH," he reiterated. "Please, for the sake of our love, do not cook any more spinach pie."

The wife beamed and, with a joyful smile, replied, "Why didn't you tell me sooner? I also hate spinach, but because you seemed to enjoy my mother's spinach pie so much on the day you came to ask for my hand in marriage, I forced myself to cook and eat it at least once a week so as not to disappoint you."

"I wish that I would have told your mother that I did not like spinach pie!" the husband declared. The couple embraced each other, laughed, and promised each other that they would never hold back anything. Instead, they would discuss everything openly and with sincerity. They acknowledged that their burden of eating **spinach pie** had been removed from their lives, and they lived happily ever after.

The seemingly inconsequential 'sticking point' had a considerable impact on the couple's relationship because each party was afraid to speak their mind. Once they communicated openly, they discovered that love always finds a way, and honest communication prevents feelings from escalating and creating unhealthy conditions.

(2) *The "You Matter" Commitment*

Everyone needs reassurance that they matter to someone, and in no instance does this come into play more than in romantic/love relationships. To let someone know every day, several times, that they matter is the ultimate form of love and respect. A demonstration of the "you matter" commitment can take the form of words and deeds.

(A) Habits and Behaviors

(1) *Commitment to Mutual Engagement in Life*

When you decide to marry or cohabitate, you must set up a plan for how you go about daily life together, from the time you awaken until you close your eyes at night. For example, if having meals together is important to you, establish a time to dine and commit to being at the table at that hour, irrespective of other plans. Do not allow other plans to interfere with that commitment, and look forward to the solidarity of the family meal. That commitment is a promise that both parties display as a sign of devotion and interest in their significant other. It says that you want to take time away from the hum-drum routine of your day and make your soul mate feel special because they matter.

If dining together is not possible due to work schedules or other concerns, consciously organize your daily plans to include each other in another way. Do something that you mutually enjoy, giving each other a sense of purpose just by being in each other's company. Mutual hobbies or engagements will make being together a joyful experience and maintain the romantic spark between you.

(2) *Learning About "Love Buttons"*

The term "love buttons" signifies those trigger points that ignite feelings of romance, love, and appreciation in your spouse or significant other. You should learn about these "buttons" early on in your relationship by asking each other direct questions about your mutual expectations of each other—namely, what activities or gestures your loved one considers to be genuine displays of love. Sometimes, the questions can be as simple as asking your soul mate how their day went and listening attentively to their responses. For others, expressions of love may take the form of performing household chores or taking care of the children; helping their soul mate with their medical care or treatment in times of need; collaborating on mutually beneficial tasks (e.g., dishwashing); or preparing your loved one's favorite meal or dessert.

In other words, "love buttons" ignite the flames of romance, bring a smile to your loved one's face and enhance your enjoyment of life together. Early in our relationship, we learned about "Love Buttons," and they guided us throughout our many years of happily married life. Looking back, we realize that we continue to add different components to make our "Love Buttons" more meaningful. "Love Buttons" should remain part of the marital conversation throughout time. Sometimes we remind each other of the Love Button we spoke about at the beginning of our marriage. Feel free to add to the list of "Love Buttons" as time passes. Each gesture improves the relationship as time goes by and cultivates a more fulfilling intimate life.

There is nothing wrong with adding other "love buttons" to your list. As we always say, it is a good practice to improve the relationship as the years pass. This is especially true because "love buttons" enable you to continue unlocking the door to intimacy. Praising and complimenting each other will also enhance your love life and the overall relationship.

Additional Love-Button Suggestions:

Consider the following additional "love-button" suggestions: Compose love songs for your soul mate and serenade her/him in romantic ways;

- *Cook dinner by candlelight with flowers on the table;*

- *Send a text or an email expressing your love romantically and sincerely;*

- *Post a sticker on the computer screen, car, door, or desk expressing the words, "I love you";*

- *Post a photo and note on one of your soul mate's social media pages;*

- *Express how much you enjoy being with your soul mate on all occasions;*

- *Create and hang a picture collage to commemorate your times together;*

- *Do not be shy to say, "I love you very much" just because you are the best thing that ever happened to me;*

- *Look for ways to praise your soul mate at all times and do not complain.*

While we are alive, we have the time to express those words, so do not hesitate. Time is of the essence.

Remember to step outside your comfort zone. If your significant other likes to do certain things that do not appeal to you, compromise and do it anyway—if it does not affect you in any way. For example, during a visit to Arizona. We remember when Esther made a remark that she wanted to go on a balloon ride. That was amazing because Esther never enjoyed taking such chances. But we went on the adventure and created a beautiful memory that gives us cause for amusement and laughter to this day whenever we speak about it.

If you're not adventurous and prefer not to try new things, show you care by periodically stepping outside your comfort zone and going that extra mile—either emotionally or physically. Remember that love is not a sacrifice at all; it is a blessing.

(3) *Validate Your Significant Other*

External validation means the world to most people and reinforces the "You Matter Commitment." Never complain about those activities and endeavors that add spice or bring joy to your loved one. Instead, support their interests and dreams (except, of course, if their desired goals are not beneficial to themselves or others). By validating your soul mate, you brighten the relationship and inspire feelings of trust, confidence, and security.

(4) *The "Matchy-Matchy" Challenge*

One way to demonstrate love and unity in front of our family, friends, and acquaintances is by making a fashion statement. We often wear the same T-shirt, matching pants, same-color or color-coordinated outfits to show that we are a couple. During the pandemic, we also try to wear matching masks. We call this practice "matchy-matchy"— We have been practicing this custom since the early stages of our marriage. It has impacted our granddaughters so much that if by any chance, we do not wear the same color coordination or wear different clothing, they remark, "What happened? Why are you two not matchy-matchy." We recommend this approach to many couples, and as soon as they start color-coordinating or wearing the same shirts, they feel that they truly belong to one another. We declare to the world that we belong to the same team. We love to see when couples expand this practice to include their children. We invite you to take the "Matchy-Matchy" challenge and experience the change it brings to your life.

(5) *Intimacy and Sexual Practices*

Intimacy and sexual practices are among the most important ways to communicate and express a couples' love for each other. God has commanded us to be fruitful and multiply, and that can only happen through sexual intercourse. At the same time, intimacy is a couple's way of communicating their needs and enjoyment throughout their lives together. Displays of deep love should be a natural consequence of the relationship, even when your children have grown and moved away from the 'nest.' Intimate practices should continue throughout time, into old age, and become as natural as other pleasurable happenings. Many claim that sexual desire begins to diminish around the age of fifty. However, with life expectancy constantly increasing, eighty is the new fifty. We know many couples who have reached or surpassed eighty, and are still enjoying each other's company and their romantic relationship.

Intimacy and sexual practices must always ignite love's flame and be a source of joy. Suppose adverse or unforeseeable circumstances cause the flame to diminish or be extinguished altogether (e.g., due to stress, illness, accident, temptations that cause the couple to separate, or other issues within your family life). In that case, we suggest that you seek ways to remedy and help one another overcome those obstacles. You may wish to seek the help of a doctor, a minister, or a counselor, but do not leave that issue aside. Also, don't become complacent and accept the situation as it is. Doing so will make both of you miserable. God wants the two of you to enjoy the fruits of your marriage and enjoy your sexual relationship into old age. Never withhold intimacy as a form of retribution or punishment or use it as a bargaining tool. Either of these behaviors will quash the flame of love and intimacy entirely.

Sex and intimacy should always be spontaneous, loving, and sincere—never an obligatory routine to be dismissed. Both of you must be in a mutual-gratification state of mind. Find ways to please each other. Sex should never be painful or uncomfortable.

(6) *Respecting Boundaries*

Relationships only thrive and endure where boundaries are present. There must be respect for each party's freedom to act and express their truths (within reason and without intentionally harming anyone).

Everyone has an inherent expectation of privacy. When your spouse tells you, "I don't want to talk about it" this typically signifies that he/she does not feel disposed to divulge any feelings now and needs to be alone. In that case, you can demonstrate support by letting him/her know that you are there for them should they require your intervention, support, or advice. It is important not to impose your will or even make suggestions unless and until you have the go-ahead to do so. The most harmful thing that any partner can do is to be sarcastic and cause the situation to worsen. Acting without your soul mate's permission may cause friction and tension between both of you.

Conversely, you must also maintain your own boundaries. If your day has not gone according to plan, you should not bring frustration or disappointment home from work. Try to resolve the issue so that your feelings do not overburden or impose upon your spouse's space or quietude. On the other hand, since communication is essential, you can broach the subject gently to determine their readiness to listen. At all times, do not take out your anger or negativity on your spouse.

Persistent tendencies to allocate blame and project dissatisfaction onto your love partner will cause severe rifts in the relationship. Therefore, if something happens outside the home to disturb or distress you— either at work, with friends, or other matters, remember to maintain your sense of reason and do not project your anger or sadness. Instead, before you reenter your home, remind yourself to remain calm by touching a tree or a symbolic wall outside your home to symbolically dispense and free yourself from the day's burdens and do so again before leaving for work. The tree will absorb your frustration—and your promise not to impose upon your soul mate and family. Remember that your spouse is there to strengthen, encourage, celebrate, embrace and console you. In times of distress, your soul mate also reminds you to maintain faith in God because there is a reason and purpose for everything. No matter what happens today, the sun will come out by the next dawn.

(7) *Apologize For Wrongdoing or Unintentional Errors*

As human beings, we are all susceptible to missteps and errors, either intentional, unintentional, or as a result of temptations that mislead us in the wrong direction. Remember that through the Law of Attraction, your thoughts and expressions will yield what you desire. At all times, when an idea or an impulse comes to your mind, use the funnel of your spirit to sift through your thoughts and feelings to determine which ones will benefit you, your loved one and your family. Embrace the good and discard the rest. When our actions impact our loved one and family negatively, the best way to remove any additional damage is to admit the mistake and amend it. Pledge that you will not allow the wrongdoing to happen again, and most significantly, ask for forgiveness. That is the most effective and just course of action. By simply acknowledging your wrongdoing and sincerely expressing regret, you cleanse your entire being and heal from the incident. In doing so, you are not displaying weakness but nobility of heart and spirit. You also pave the way for self-improvement by understanding where you went wrong and learning to prevent recurrences of that behavior. That will result in the spiritual victory that all of us seek in the world.

(8) *Avoid Jealousy*

One of the most common offenders in a relationship is jealousy. Jealousy is the manifestation of insecurity based on a distorted reality. Jealous people entertain so much self-doubt that they project their feelings onto their spouses or others, creating a domino effect of resentment and bitterness. A loss of control also accompanies feelings of insecurity. (For example, if your spouse receives a promotion or commendation at work, you may feel diminished in some sense—as though you were unworthy of the same level of recognition.) However, these feelings are phantoms—ghosts of self-consciousness and doubt that never disappear and tend to follow your spouse everywhere. Tell yourself, again and again, "These ghosts are not real. They must be gone now! I will not allow feelings of diminished self-worth to destroy our harmonious relationship."

By demonstrating your love as a unified whole, you reinforce the "You Matter" Commitment.

CHAPTER 4

FAMILY LIFE—BUILDING YOUR WORLD TOGETHER

Once you have found your soul mate, you should make all your decisions together as a unified whole, in consultation with each other, harmoniously, and with joy. In creating your lives as one, you have the opportunity to build a life together founded on the principles of love, understanding via communication, commitment, and establishing one family. From the moment both of you join in matrimony, separation ends. The term and concept of "family" signify one unit (not "your family" and "my family).

Below, we present some suggestions for the successful creation of your new environment as spouses. Once both of you commit to following some or all of our suggestions in this text, you will discover how beautiful life is as a married couple. You go from physical attraction to friendship to love, sex and intimacy. Then, as time passes, you become so bonded that you cannot imagine your lives apart. Soon, you finish one another's sentences, choose the same restaurants and vacation spots. These are the priceless gifts of married life.

(A) *Establish Your Circle of Love and Build On Your Circle of Life*

You and your soul mate are joining together and will carry on some of the legacies that each of your family provided to you while growing up. That may seem like a tremendous responsibility, but in truth, building on the legacies of our ancestors is the ultimate honor.

But you also have the chance to begin new traditions of your own in your Circle of Love that you may want to carry into your Circle of Life. Your Circle of Life comprises your extended families, co-workers, acquaintances, or friends you have not encountered yet.

In establishing your Circle of Life, both of you must agree on your practices and methods. At times, your extended family and friends might disrupt the flow of this process by trying to impose their influence and options. They might even make unproductive, hurtful remarks to derail your mutual agreements. Both of you must be very aware of the circumstances surrounding you and protect your Circle of Love—the most sacred blessing the two of you have together. Your Circle of Love consists of you, your spouse, and your children. It also includes the practices and behaviors that you seek to cultivate. The circles can comingle at different times, and the more people you allow into your life, the more the circles expand.

By establishing your Circles of Love and Life, you begin creating new patterns and practices that constitute your world and family and must occur without abandoning your family traditions and customs. In our *TLC For Couples* book, we suggested that each couple write down the ground rules for educating your children, raising them in a particular faith, methods for handling your finances, and other essential matters that you must address as a unit.

(B) *Write Down Your Mutual Goals and Bucket Lists*

Writing a bucket list is one of the most important things you need to do as a couple. It also enables both of you to bond with each other, solidify your union, and create lasting memories. Do not be afraid to dream big. Do not worry about costs or how and when the dreams will take shape. Remember that the universe is listening to all your wishes and well-intentioned desires and making them appear before you—like a genie, saying, "Your wish is my command." You will have things to look forward to as a married couple; your mutual goals will keep you on course and focused if hectic schedules, commitments, and pressures tend to obscure the significance of "us" and spending time together. It will also maintain mutual engagement in pleasurable activities.

The lists should detail the activities that you enjoy individually and together to enhance your quality of life. As we mentioned earlier, it is essential to think outside the box and give your spouse free rein to do the same. Although you may have differences in opinion about the definition of "fun," allow yourself to compromise, understand and validate every goal and dream your spouse entertains and make them your own—especially if they make your soul mate happy.

Employ such a profound level of supportiveness that things you never envisioned become part of your life plan. Doing so will emotionally and physically expand your horizon. Remember that giving up something you enjoy for the sake of compromising with your spouse is not sacrifice but the act of lovingly embracing the "You Matter" commitment.

Never negate or downplay your soul mate's dream. When you look at the proper spelling of the word 'impossible,' you can see the affirmation, **"I'M POSSIBLE."** If you are in unison and sync, *everything* is possible.

We recall the time we traveled to Sydney, Australia, to visit the Sydney Jewish Museum. We purchased a book entitled " *Nothing Is Impossible"* by Gabriel Kune. The book chronicles the life of John Saunders, the museum's founder. Mr. Saunders was a Holocaust survivor; he worked hard, employed his vast intellect, charitable and philanthropic natures. He was an incredibly positive person, famous for his expression, "nothing is impossible." Saunders became a billionaire by age sixty-four and enjoyed enormous success in his later years. Not only did he build the Holocaust Museum to memorialize the massacre of six million Jews and five million others, but he donated enough to the museum to preserve the landmark for many years to come.

(C) *Utilize God's Personal Service (GPS) As Your Family Guide*

When facing difficulties, "GPS"(God's Personal Service—our term) is a tool that is always available to you. Now that you have wed or are planning to marry, this compass will be essential on your journey to marital harmony and joy.

Utilizing "GPS" is a tool that enables us to tap into God's wisdom and select the appropriate program tailored to your preferences. Through prayer, you can selectively ask God for what you want to happen in your family's life. No matter how complex or straightforward the request may be, when you connect your channel to the energy that God gives you and invite the Creator to be your guide as you navigate life's pathways, your load becomes much easier to carry. When you encounter bumps and tribulations, sometimes they are the Creator's voice telling you to withstand your trials. Soon you will emerge into the light and consider other opportunities that God wants you to observe—open doors to endless possibilities.

We always worked together to build our business. Even as newlyweds, we experienced many trials and tests. At times, it seemed as though our world was about to cave in, but by using the GPS, we discovered that the outcome exceeded our expectations.

Every detour is a lesson in the gift of choices, and your family will benefit even (and maybe *especially*) from the rocky roads that could lead to unexpected opportunities. Placing your faith in God and using the "GPS" awakens you to new vistas of discovery that you may never have imagined. Just keep the channels open and allow your initiative and flow of ideas to guide you to your destination.

You can never imagine how beautiful life together can be unless you take the plunge and experience it.

(D) *Wedding Tips*

Your wedding day must be one of the most memorable experiences of your lifetime. Therefore, it can be daunting to plan for an event of that magnitude. But remember that your special occasion memorializing your love is more about you than the preparations and ceremonial activities. Take time to pay attention to each other while planning for the big day.

Since the pandemic, wedding venues, like other businesses, have suffered. But we will invest our faith in a plague-free future, where all of us can be together and rejoice in such momentous occasions.

Below, we offer some suggestions that might help you get through the hectic days leading up to your nuptials. As you proceed, engage in compromise at all times. Remember to act as a unified whole. Never make a unilateral decision or allow your family or friends to direct your plans. Doing so causes disharmony in your relationship and the family. This is your big day, and the couple must make the final decisions about the wedding's location, the number of invited guests, your choice of music, and the menu. When we got married fifty-seven years ago, we were teenagers without independent financial resources. However, we made every decision together. Although our wedding was simple, we made it look lavish.

(1) *Time and Season*

Choosing the time and season of your wedding is most important. Doing so will set the stage for every other task as you go along. Timing matters because it provides your wedding's backdrop. Ask yourselves whether you want a winter, spring, fall, or summer wedding. Although most couples wed in the summertime, most venues are booked in the warmer months, and you must act quickly to secure a place. One note to consider: Off-season weddings may be more budget-friendly than peak-season celebrations. The sight of colors turning in fall or the enchantment of a winter landscape can be just as beautiful as the balmy days of spring and summer.

Take your time and think about the backdrop of your wedding. Will it be autumn foliage, a winter wonderland, or a paradisiacal spring/summer garden?

(2) *Venue/Ambience*

The wedding venue is an essential consideration for celebrating your union. It comprises the backdrop and the epicenter of fun and celebration for the couple and their guests. Choose the venue carefully and ask yourselves what type of ambiance you prefer, whether outdoors, indoors, or a combination of both for the ceremony and reception. Discuss whether you want a formal or a casual wedding with an elegant or more formal theme? Do you want overnight accommodations for your guests? Travel conveniences (such as shuttles to and from airports) typically will be available at the venue of your choice. Most venues offer meal preparations or recommend reputable outside vendors. Some even provide onsite gourmet chefs and delicious cuisine.

(3) *Wedding Planners*

Never dismiss the priceless worth of a wedding planner. When you delegate the task of planning your wedding to a professional, all of your stress will disappear. Wedding planners have a keen sense of what you will require on your special day and how to maximize time efficiency. Preliminarily, they will sit down with you and discuss the details of your wedding and tailor every aspect of the reception to your needs and styles. Feel free to communicate with them, and don't hold back when conceptualizing and expressing your vision. Expert wedding planners often present you with package deals that provide for the venue, meals, guest accommodations, and preparations that lead up to the day of your wedding so that you can be hassle-free. When required, they also can refer you to reputable outside vendors.

Remember: The Law of Attraction applies as much to wedding planning as every other engagement.

(4) *The Menu*

One of the essential aspects of wedding planning is the menu. Some couples prefer to honor their respective traditions and cultures with their choice of culinary fare. They may also wish to consider various alternatives, including vegan and vegetarian meals for their guests.

In the latter case, you might also wish to visit https://sarasorganiceats.com/ for some delicious ideas to include on your menu—and in your daily meal preparation.

(5) *The Cake*

The wedding cake, like the menu, can be tailored to your unique personalities, preferences, and styles. When choosing your cake, it's best to rely on an expert who comes recommended either by your wedding planner or someone you trust within your family and friends. Don't be shy to communicate your vision that expresses your love's sweetness and the days of happy matrimony ahead. You may wish to bring photos or drawings to demonstrate your ideas.

(6) *The Guest List/Seating Arrangements*

As you celebrate your love, you want to have your closest family and friends around you. In preparing the guest list, the delicate issue of who should be added or omitted can cause significant unrest. Try to avoid such tension by limiting the list to those in your immediate Circle of Love and Life.

Also, when considering the seating arrangements, preservation of harmony is of paramount importance. You want your guests to feel comfortable and joyful throughout the entire event. Therefore, employ as much discretion as possible in seating your guests.

(7) *Gifts/The Bridal Registry*

Gifts are a way of showing appreciation for the bride and groom. However, as with other considerations, buying for the couple should be an easy, enjoyable process. Many brides register at their favorite stores and shops to provide their guests with innovative gift ideas. Some invitees prefer creating homemade presents as a sign of affection and regard for the couple; others opt to give monetary gifts. But the most beautiful and lasting form of recognition is your guests' presence at your ceremony and reception.

(8) *The Attire*

Couples, don't forget to begin shopping for your wedding attire early on. Dresses and tuxedos must be an expression of yourselves. Don't be afraid to make a fashion statement. Are you elegant and sedate or unique and trendy? Allow yourself to shine—your way.

(9) *The Rings*

The wedding rings not only review your sense of taste but, more significantly, your commitment to each other as a couple. Consider having the rings engraved with a profound declaration of your love, another reminder of "forever." When we got married, we adapted the custom that we carry on for all these years. Before we go to sleep, we kiss each other's rings to remind us of our commitment that will endure throughout eternity.

(10) *The Vows*

Whether you have a religious or secular ceremony, your vows should be the most profound declaration of your love for each other. Vows can be either traditional or personalized to convey your feelings and the significance of the moment. If you wish to write your own vows, give yourself time to contemplate what your fiancé(e) means to you. Recall the day you met and how your life has changed since that time. Reflect on how your fiancé(e) has enhanced your life and his/her unique attributes. If emotion overwhelms you or you feel 'stuck,' ask for help from a loved one, a trusted friend, or a professional writer who can compose your text for you. In the latter instance, the hired professional will interview you briefly to determine your thoughts and sentiments and magically craft them into the perfect verbal manifestation of your heart. In this instance, be sure to review and personalize the text. There is nothing more meaningful than expressing your inner feelings that will remain forever.

(11) *Avoid Do-It-Yourself, Last-Minute Preparations*

No matter how you choose to prepare for or spend your day, have fun and do not allow yourself to become trapped in the details. Whenever possible, delegate to those you trust and celebrate each other. Attempting the Do-It-Yourself ("DIY") approach tends to generate stress and, often, causes unnecessary confusion. Instead, relax, enjoy the moment, engage in self-care, and create memories to last a lifetime.

Make your wedding day the most memorable, enduring declaration of love.

(E) *Honeymoon Preparations—Suggestions*

Preparing for your honeymoon can be as daunting as wedding arrangements, and you must be careful not to stress or exert yourself unnecessarily. Below, we present a few tips that might assist you on your journey as you celebrate your marriage.

(1) *Researching*

We refer to step one as "researching" because, as with all endeavors, knowledge serves as the conceptual vehicle that transports you where you want to go. Choose a destination that appeals to both of you and select a theme. Perhaps, you enjoy adventures in the outdoors, such as hiking, frequenting beaches, parks, or nature trails. If so, be mindful of the season, wear proper clothing and footwear, and be sure to pace yourself.

On the other hand, you may prefer indoor engagements, such as concerts, theater, or lecture series. In that case, be sure to take such items as your phone and video cameras and a note-taking device (possibly a laptop) to record or write down your experience and etch your special moments in time.

(2) *Book Your Destination As Soon As Possible*

Booking early ensures a place for you in the venue of your choice and alleviates the burden of last-minute preparation. Because peak-season bookings often lead to disappointments, it is best to secure your reservation early, especially if you intend to travel overseas. (Also inquire about vaccination and visa requirements.) In that way, you can be sure that your preferences will be available.

(4) *Know the Landscape*

When planning a trip, "winging it" never works. You must understand and familiarize yourself with the region of your choice and the options at your disposal. Specifically, before you leave, try to research the landscape and the most common transportation methods in a given area. For example, make sure that you have maps and other directional tools on hand to navigate your surroundings. Get to know bus routes, train schedules, or rent-a-car options. You don't want to find yourself in the middle of nowhere without a plan.

(5) *Organize Your Itinerary*

Once you are at least reasonably comfortable with the landscape, organize your game plan. Make a schedule of places to visit and note the landmarks. For example, if you visit landmarks in New York, schedule specific dates for visiting the Statue of Liberty or the Freedom Tower. Spontaneity can be exciting, but if you travel to a place for the first time or are from a small town and unused to a large metropolis, you can get lost—geographically and otherwise.

(6) *Keep the Home-Fires Burning*

When you leave home, make sure that a trusted family member, neighbor, or friend will look after your house, pet family members, and personal effects. The sanctuary of your home is your haven and must be preserved at all times, as must the well-being of your pet family members who anxiously await your return.

(7) *Watch Your Pocket Before and After Your Trip*

The excitement of your new life together as a couple may sometimes cloud your sense of prudence. Creating memories to last a lifetime requires money, but be sure to gauge your spend-thriftiness according to your means. Work out a mutually beneficial budget together. You can have the time of your life but always be mindful of your pocket. Most significantly, when you travel, make sure that both of you carry money with you. If currencies vary, credit cards may be useful, but many vendors may not accept that payment method. Consider the currency exchange fee and the difference in the exchange rate when you complete the transaction. When you purchase an item, someone might tell you that the cost in dollars is $50.00, but when you return home, you discover that you paid more than the quoted price.

Be sure to guard your wallets and handbags if you are on tour or in a shopping mall. Be alert at all times— but do not be fearful. Cherish the moments. Everything that you experience on your honeymoon or vacation will create memories that last a lifetime.

One memorable example from our own cherished memory bank occurred in 1964 when we went to Atlantic City on our honeymoon. Before we left, we counted all our monetary wedding gifts and put aside the reserve. Then we decided to use the rest to create lasting memories. I (Mordechai) wanted to be the perfect gentleman and was eager to purchase everything Esther admired.

One day, we went for a walk around the boardwalk and stopped in several stores along the way. Esther loved a bathing suit in the window display, and we went in and bought it. She was delighted. Then we bought some souvenirs that we still have today. We also went into an electronic store, and the excellent salesman guided us in purchasing a radio with all the gimmicks at a great price. At that time, this type of radio was the latest model. The salesperson demonstrated all the radio's specifications and capabilities with a floor model. Sadly, that experience taught us an expensive lesson. We did not open the box until we arrived home— like enthusiastic children receiving the holiday gifts of their dreams. First, we inserted the batteries and turned on the radio. *Here we go! Oh, no! Think again.* The radio only played FM stations and was static.

The motto of the story: Never take anything at face value. Examine all your purchases before you take them home.

(8) *Be Carefree*

Last but not least, enjoy yourself! This time in your life will never come again, and if you plan pragmatically and reasonably, you will have an unforgettable experience. Like the wedding, the honeymoon is a memorialization of your love, and that is what makes it so meaningful.

Make your honeymoon a memorable experience.

(F) Family Planning

Family planning is not only determined by the number of children you and your spouse decide to raise and nurture. The 'plan' has to be a mutual decision that involves thinking ahead about the responsibilities that the decision carries. After all, you will become a co-creator by bringing a new life into the world.

When planning a family, you commit to being part of a unit—something greater than yourself. However, your role as an integral component of that unit is irreplaceable. Everyone has a place within the Circle of Love, and when one person suspends or negates their responsibility, the whole operation ceases to function.

(1) *Take Time to Listen and Be In the Moment*

Your family is the bedrock of your entire life. Nothing comes close in importance. Therefore, as committed as you are to your job, family beckons you in ways that your professional life cannot.

Therefore, it is essential to balance and prioritize your family as the foremost consideration in your world. You cannot detach from your family as you disconnect from electronic devices. When addressing each member of your family, embrace and appreciate their humanity. Listen, learn, gently advise, and guide them as valued, treasured family members. After all, that is what they are.

Your daughter's ballet recital or play and your son's musical concert or sports engagement are far more meaningful than any email or spreadsheet. These moments will never come again.

On their deathbed, no one has ever asked for their last text or direct message. People want to see their sons, daughters, or nearest relatives at every stage of the journey.

(2) *Express Love*

Don't be shy about expressing love—often. You have only one lifetime. Whether you do so in words or actions, make sure that you demonstrate your devotion and love for each member of your family. In doing so, respect and acknowledge the different ways in which they show their love for you—express gratitude for their presence as the most precious aspect of your life.

Bestow the gift of your presence by detaching from work during off-hours. Put away all electronic devices at the meal table and engage in conversation. Speak about your day and ask your loved ones to do the same.

Take time to ask meaningful questions and give of your heart. If someone needs your advice, offer it in the form of suggestions. Imposing or demanding will cause tension. Narrate a story or experience that you lived in your youth, ensuring that you provide loving, caring input with meaningful examples. Most people will remember the story that you told them for many years to come.

As you give, receive graciously. Seek advice with humility and trust that those you love will come through for you. Work together for each other's highest good.

(3) *Remember Significant Dates*

Anniversaries, birthdays, and other special occasions are momentous events that parents, including children and other family members, must never miss. It is essential that the male—even more than the female remembers and takes time to remember special dates and milestones. Don't allow excuses to get in the way. There is nothing more significant than seeing a family member smile with joy because you have taken the time and have made an effort to pay tribute and offer praise.

And as we mentioned earlier, you don't have to wait for an occasion to express love and acknowledgment. The act of bestowing love with a message, email, post, or any other gesture must be an everyday occurrence that helps the family thrive and prosper with happiness, peace, and harmony. For example, you can tell your spouse in a message to remember that this weekend is your parents' anniversary, and you need to plan for the occasion. Also, remember to remind your spouse of your child's upcoming birthday. These are building blocks that enhance the relationship and take it to the next level. Be careful not to make arrogant or sarcastic remarks when presenting such a beautiful suggestion. That will destroy the entire purpose and create disharmony in your relationship.

(4) *Write a Family Mission Statement*

A family mission statement is a doctrine or code of conduct that every member must follow—much like a corporation that sets the standard for its CEOs and employees. The credo helps define the common goals that each member sets and works to achieve for the good of the whole.

Below is a sample mission statement that you might wish to incorporate into your family's daily life.

We, the _____ (family name), pledge to each other, individually and collectively, that we will faithfully and lovingly engage in the following practices:

(1) Express and demonstrate love and respect;
(2) Display gratitude for each other;
(3) Cherish time spent together;

(4) Listen before speaking;
(5) Be considerate of each other's individual needs;
(6) Come to the table during mealtime and converse (without checking phones or tablets);
(7) Follow the designated rules and chores as established by parents or other family members without complaint;
(8) Offer counsel and advice when requested without making demands;
(9) Offer comfort to others in times of distress;
(10) Accept advice graciously and humbly;
(11) Remember and participate in special occasions without offering excuses for failure to do so; offer acknowledgment on 'ordinary days' as well.
(12) Always end controversial discussions in compromise;
(13) Commit to maintaining harmony;
(14) Begin and end the day with a smile.
(15) Become a problem solver, not a problem creator.

The above is a suggested list of behaviors and practices to guide you on your way. As individuals, each family is unique and beautiful. Understand and celebrate those qualities together and spread joy and love wherever you go. Be a living, breathing manifestation of the values you share.

(G) Help Your Children with Their Personal Growth

(1) *Lead By Example*

Parents typically want their children to establish their own personalities and traits to create their unique blueprint in the world. However, growing children need guidance—a sense of security in emulating those they most admire. No one can provide that stability more effectively than parents who genuinely care and seek the good of their family.
Each individual must have a solid foundation on which to grow and mature. The building blocks of development are:

- Love
- Understanding
- Kindness
- Compassion
- Discernment
- Good Humor
- Wisdom (developed over time, through experience, that you share with others)
- A belief system by which you live

The most significant task any parent has is to infuse these ideas into their children by demonstrating them through expression and action.

Take a deep, honest look at yourself, and you will see who your children will become. If you are kind and considerate, the chances are that you will pass these qualities on to your children. If, on the other hand, you are argumentative and have a pessimistic worldview, you will transfer your perspectives (however unconsciously) to your offspring. Therefore, maintaining an awareness of self and understanding how you are projecting yourself around others is vital to cultivating the next generation.

Keep in mind that each person comes with his or her own soul and has a mission to fulfill in this world. No matter what kind of influences we have around us, each individual grows to be their own person. The most important thing that each parent can do is to set a good foundation. The rest is up to each one of the children.

(2) *Provide Structure and Guidance*

Providing structure and guidance to your children involves setting boundaries and behavioral guidelines (see our suggested Family Mission Statement, above). Doing so is much like selecting the standards for a governing body. Each person in the hierarchy has a set of rules and regulations they must follow so that the entire administration can function smoothly.

Individuals must have responsibilities within the family structure to not place undue burdens on a few; everyone must work together in harmony without hesitation or complaint. Each individual must respect the roles of others in the 'system.'

Respect and love are the guiding principles that keep every organization running. The family is the most enduring and valued 'institution' in our society—the bedrock of nations and the world.

(3) *Validate and Compliment*

As mentioned earlier, everyone needs to know that they mean the world to someone. **When you validate, you elevate.** Compliments will never 'spoil' your children. Instead, when children learn and observe that their parents value their actions and behaviors, they will be motivated to pursue that goal or practice. The gifts of love and validation continue to give and thrive throughout generations. As they seek and gain parental approval, children will acquire the tools and inspiration to nurture their children, and the family unit will thrive for years to come.

(4) *Understand Detours*

At times, parents' vision for their children does not match their children's goals or expectations. In that case, parents should understand that although there may be a detour in objectives, the most crucial consideration is the children's happiness (as long as their choice is reasonable and ultimately for their benefit). For example, many parents want their children to pursue lucrative professions (e.g., law or medicine) and discourage more creative engagements, such as theater or the arts. If the children have a genuine aptitude for one or another profession, they begin to map out a life of their choosing. Go with that and support their decision with all your heart. We have only one life, and there is no turning back. Financial comfort is usually an outgrowth of loving one's chosen path.

(5) *Reflect and Release*

Once you, as a parent, have nurtured, validated, and supported your child through the growing process, sit back and rejoice! Release your worry and concern and allow negativity to glide away on seasonal breezes. You *never* stop being a parent—even when your child becomes an adult. However, once you have set the foundation, you can enjoy the rewards of your efforts. You now become their co-creator in joy and can reflect on the lessons given, learned, and passed down to successive generations.

(H) Divorce

What happens when irreconcilable differences threaten the marital bond? The question is not one we ever want to contemplate. The terms "divorce" and "separation" must not enter the couple's vocabulary or be a means of 'finding a way out' of the marriage.

Marriage requires work, and the road will not always be without stumbling blocks. The purpose of marriage is the ability to resolve issues together as a united front. That includes casting away stones, rebuilding, and recalibrating your course when things don't go according to plan.

If the issues cause your disagreement to seem overwhelming, seek marriage counseling before resorting to divorce or separation. Rewind and reflect on your traits, habits, and personalities that brought you together and ignited the initial attraction. Rekindle your former feelings of bliss in the 'fantasy phase'; work through your differences with respect and love for each other as a couple and individuals.

If the above suggestions do not work for both of you and the objective intervention of a professional counselor or your clergy does not guide you on course, seek a second chance at love and part ways amicably, especially if there are children in your family. Both of you must agree on how you will explain the matter to your children. Always affirm that your separation has nothing to do with them. Emphasize that you love all of them equally and will always be there for them even though you do not live together.

There is always an opportunity to begin anew and create a New Circle of Love. Open your heart to new possibilities, and learn from your mistakes. Possibly, you did not have a chance to employ the practices suggested in this book and could not remedy the issues that led to your separation or divorce (such as the failure to share your problems with each other, work out your financial challenges together, or other family issues); or perhaps you have allowed outside influences from family and friends to disrupt your thoughts and sense of peace.

If you ultimately decide to separate, you will find that many of the issues you confronted as a couple will resurface with a new partner.

We undertook the task of writing this book for that specific reason. God inspired us to write and enlighten couples on how to live happily, peacefully, and successfully for many years on earth and into eternity.

No one should have to feel trapped in unpleasant—or even toxic—circumstances. Just be sure to maintain and keep your belief in love alive!

Nothing is final, and you are the ultimate architect of your destiny. As long as you live, you have a chance to complete your mission and enjoy the life that God intended you to live. Follow your faith in God and let 'GPS' guide your life.

When traveling through life, your 'GPS' is the most effective compass for guiding you toward success and happiness.

CONCLUSION—FINAL THOUGHTS AND SYNOPSIS

The path to personal and marital success and happiness lies within you. In this book, we have demonstrated how you can create a lifetime of fulfillment. We pray that both of you and your souls have been touched by the examples and suggestions that God has allowed us to provide in this book. We also pray that your family and friends will notice the difference in you and will want to read this book, as well, to enlighten and guide them in their personal and marital life.

To summarize:

The first step begins with understanding yourself, establishing a connection to who you are through personal reflection and meditation, and cleansing the cobwebs of your past—even when doing so is painful.

Contemplate the divine pattern of the universe and your life, and allow yourself to be guided by 'GPS.'

Live with "an attitude of gratitude," embrace your challenges and reach out to others with love, compassion, kindness, and respect. Adapt the Law of Attraction to your life's vision and dreams, and witness the magic that the universe has in store for you. Envision, employ initiative, act, and rejoice in the outcome.

Live each day in expectation of your dreams' manifestation and create a "Bucket List" of things you most enjoy.

When you have found your true self, you are ready to begin a new chapter with your soul mate. Know that males and females may have different approaches to life, and that is perfectly acceptable. Diversity of thought and action makes the world go around and adds spice to life.

Establish your relationship based on respect, trust, open communication, and compromise. Let your soul mate feel validated at all times and let them know that they matter.

As you establish your Circles of Love and List, write down your mutual "Bucket Lists" and support each other's goals, using 'GPS' to guide you.

Treasure moments, be there for your family with a listening ear and an open heart.

At all times, express love freely and be *in the moment* without diverting your attention to other preoccupations when you are with your family. Making memories should be an everyday, all-seasonal event.

Remember important dates and be there for those priceless moments that may never come again (e.g., a ballet recital, graduations, birthdays, etc.)

Write a family mission statement and stick to it. Each family member is an essential component of the whole.

As a parent, lead by example, advise without being pedantic, validate your children, support their dreams, and rejoice in their accomplishments.

If differences of opinions threaten to break the marital bond, find ways to rekindle your love. Remind yourselves of the qualities that initially attracted you to each other, and employ the attributes of validation, praise, and compromise. Take time to review your past and focus your energy on dismissing all negativity that you may have felt toward each other. Then, walk into forgiveness and reconciliation, embrace, and vow to love each other.

Seek objective outside counsel if resolving your issues becomes too stressful, and if none of these techniques prove effective, part ways amicably with a firm belief in the power of love and your ability to reach out for second chances.

The suggestions that we offer in this book stem from a genuine love for our readers. Our perspectives are profoundly personal but can be adapted to any individual or couple at their discretion. Love begets love, and that is the essence of our message.

Please be sure to follow our "TLC" series of publications and visit our website at www.makelifeasuccess.com to listen to our song lyrics and leave comments.

The highest form of praise is passing on the messages and recommending this book for others' benefit.

Amen.

We welcome your thoughtful feedback.

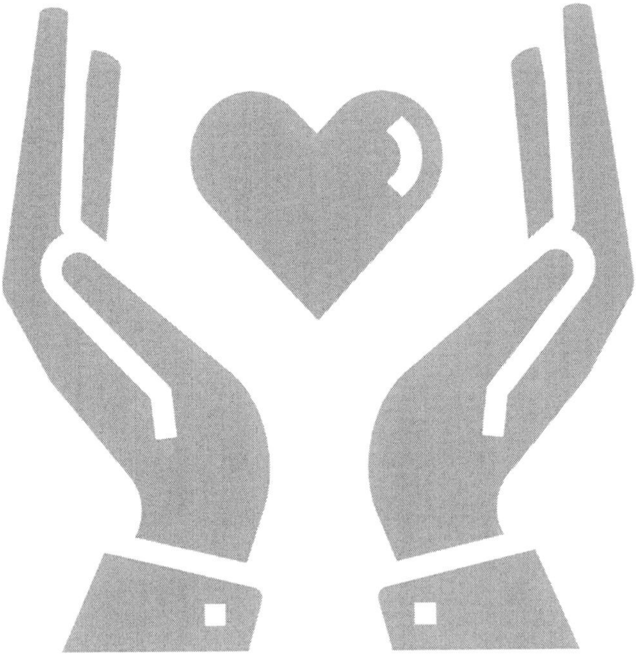

THE GRATITUDE PRAYER

Dear God,

Thank you for giving me the opportunity to open my eyes today. I know that this day will never come again, and I want to give thanks for your creation. I also appreciate and embrace each opportunity that you place before me.

I will not compare today to yesterday, because I know that each day brings a different blessing and the various experiences you send my way. I realize that you only intend to present me with challenges that teach me life lessons and give me the knowledge to understand each each day's tests. I will accept today, with all its blessings and challenges.

I realize that I must allow you to guide me with your GPS. I will accept all outcomes because I know that everything happens in your time and Divine order.

I also understand that everything happens for the best.

MORDECHAI AND ESTHER'S ROMANTIC PLAYLIST:

God Created You to Be — Mordechai and Esther Fintz
55th Anniversary Song— Mordechai and Esther Fintz
I Want to be an Angel — Mordechai and Esther Fintz
Little Things Mean a Lot — Sung by Edith Lindenman and Carl Slutz

Original Compositions at: makelifeasuccess.com.

Too Young — Nat King Cole (our wedding song)
(https://www.youtube.com/watch?v=KaFtsqU2V6U)

Unforgettable — Nat King Cole
(https://www.youtube.com/watch?v=aXjdMV7SOfE)

You Are So Beautiful To Me — Joe Cocker
(https://www.youtube.com/watch?v=WvAr9umnZ54)
(Everything I Do) I Do It For You — Bryan Adams
(https://www.youtube.com/watch?v=Y0pdQU87dc8)

It's Impossible — Perry Como (https://www.youtube.com/watch?v=BKQ9--_ZgB4)

Love Will Keep Us Together—Captain and Tennille (https://www.youtube.com/watch?v=_QNEf9oGw8o)

Roses Are Red (My Love)—Bobby Vinton (https://www.youtube.com/watch?v=8rjPC7-JMUM)

Join our mailing list! www.makelifeasuccess.com

Interact and communicate with us. We welcome your feedback, thoughts, recommendations and impressions.

ABOUT OUR LOGO

The two circles represent the ring that we continue to wear proudly since the day we took our vows. The circle signifies our love's unending wholeness. When God unified our lives, that commitment was meant to last on earth into eternity. The two flamingos in the center represent us, forming a heart that unifies us inside the Circle of Love, surrounded by the Circle of Life. They also symbolize our connection and union of two hearts as one that enables us to make our life a success.

Made in the USA
Middletown, DE
06 February 2024